the Gift of the Tithe

Acknowledgments

This book has been an exciting adventure and learning experience, but it would not have happened without the advice and discernment of the following people:

Robert Hasley, founding Pastor of St. Andrew Methodist Church was a friend and an example of unconditional love that permeates my home even now after his passing. He became a very good friend and mentor by his grace in living and in his love for all. He was a remarkable man.

This book was the inspiration of Rev. Arthur Jones, successor to Robert at St. Andrew. His efforts have made our church a beacon and blessing for North Texas. Good things are happening under his leadership and meaningful teaching. I wrote this book because he told me to write a book on tithing. His words sparked an interest and desire I didn't know I had. I thank him for the spark that now is a flame in me to write. Thank you, Arthur.

Bob Shank, of the Master Program (now Priority Living) gave me the Biblical inspiration and teaching to start my firm and to further focus my life on Christ. His teaching gave me the courage to take that step.

This book took nearly 2 years to reach the form you are reading. Necessarily, it impacted my availability for my family. My patient and discerning wife, Carol, was my sharpest editor and critic. Indeed, as in everyday life, she was usually right. Thank you, Carol. My family, Colin and Ashley, Caleb and Claire, and Jon and Callie, all offered good suggestions during the editing process. I am blessed to have all of you in my life.

This book has been influenced by many people of God who have influenced me. Billy Graham, Colonel Robert B. Thieme Jr., Pastor Creflo Dollar, Joyce Meyers and Joel Osteen have all poured into my life.

Finally, I thank you, the reader, who must have a reason for wanting to study this topic. Please take time to consider Malachi 3:10 (the cornerstone of my tithing and this book), Proverbs 19:17, and Ephesians 3:20-21. I pray those verses bless you like they have me.

Daniel R. Crain

the Gift of the Tithe

How to Find Joy
by Giving Away Your Money

Plano, Texas

Table of Contents

What Is This Book About?

First, dear reader, thank you for opening this book. This has been a labor of love, and I have been richly blessed and humbled to write it. My prayer is that you enjoy the read and absorb the content.

In the Greek language, there are two contrasting words: *gnosis* and *epignosis*. We get the word "hypnosis" from the same root word and "know" comes from there as well. Gnosis means "I hear what you are saying. I understand completely the four corners of your statements. I just don't buy it. It has no impact on me or my life." *Epignosis* means, "I hear what you are saying. I understand completely the four corners of your statement, and it has impacted me. I am internalizing your content. I am adjusting my thinking to accommodate this information, and I am applying it to how I live my life."

I pray that this information will lead you to *epignosis*.

Why do I want this information to change your life? Several reasons:

1. God loves you. God loves you so much He sent His Son to die for you so that you could have a right relationship with Him, now and for eternity. I hope this fact will be seen on every page of this book.

2. This book will hopefully show you the path not only to salvation, but how to live a more abundant, blessed life while you are here on Earth. This book isn't just about money (although money is a big part of this discussion) but about

all areas of your life, such as health, family, peace of mind, and strength against adversity.

3. Ultimately, this is a book about faith. God does not need your money. The streets of heaven are paved in gold (Revelation 21:21). What excites Him into acting in your life is faith. Tithing is an excellent way to demonstrate your faith, to greatly please God, and to be blessed in return, exceedingly and abundantly above and beyond anything you could ask or think, according to the power that lives inside of you (Ephesians 3:20). That power is faith.

This book explores the proper place for tithing in the Old and New Testaments and how this understanding coincides with Paul's statement of giving "not grudgingly or of necessity" because "God loves a cheerful giver" (2 Corinthians 9:7 NKJV). It is my assertation that there is a place for both.

Let me make this clear: You are not compelled to tithe in the New Testament age. What I am saying is that if you tithe, by faith and not from compulsion, God will reward you according to the standard of Malachi 3:10. That promise has never changed.

I have seen this in my life. My faith in His word has been richly rewarded in innumerable ways, not just financially. Tithing has been a strong point of contact between God and me for 30 years. It is not done because He commands it. Rather, it is been done from faith, and faith is always rewarded. In the process of developing these themes and others, you will get a clear picture of these items playing out in my life. My situation is no doubt unique to me, but the principles of tithing, or giving the first 10% of your income, are universal and available to all.

The book's title, *The Gift of the Tithe: How to Find Joy by Giving Away Your Money*, emphasizes the joy and anticipation of giving to the Lord. He promises a return, a blessing for those who tithe.

All this is true, but it is more than that. It is the confidence that you are doing God's will, believing in His promises described in this book, and knowing, from your relationship with Him, that by faith, you are pleasing Him and that your life will be enriched, even more than you are giving away.

It is not a *this for that* situation. You are not helping God meet payroll. What you are doing is tangibly communicating to God your love, your faith, and your confidence in His word. This communicates your appreciation and honoring of Him. When you tithe, it demonstrates that you respect Him, much like what will be seen in Abraham. It isn't a requirement but when given in faith and adoration to the Supreme God of the Universe, fulfilling His word, you are blessed, and He is pleased, not because of the money but because you are relying on Him and recognizing His importance in your life. He loves that!

Here is how the book is laid out: The text starts with the Old Testament with Cain and Abel and the first mention of giving found in the Bible. It proceeds to Noah, then Abraham, Isaac and Jacob, Moses and the Levitical Law. From there, we will spend some more time in the Old Testament when tithing was required by the Law.

Then, we move into the New Testament and observe Jesus during His incarnation on Earth. This leads to some contrasts between the Old Testament Law and Jesus' introduction of grace, while continuing to live under the Law all His earthly life.

Finally, there are some insights into how and why to use tithing in your life as a New Testament believer, even though, under grace, it is no longer required. Still, it is my assertion that it really helps.

This book is dedicated to answering the question "why tithe?" with several sidetracks along the way. You as a Christian do not tithe under compulsion. That said, as you experience tithing and God's fulfillment of His promise to you regarding tithing, you will experience a greater depth to your faith and overall wellbeing. You might end up more relaxed about your finances as you come to realize He is the one in charge of your finances. Perhaps that reliance on God and His promises will permeate your entire existence and relationships. Further, I fully expect tithing will bring you closer to God the Father and give you a deeper love of Jesus and the magnificent work and guidance in your life by the Holy Spirit.

I am not wrong about the expected impact tithing can have in your life.

Let's Start with Some Basics

This book is based on the following premises: that Jesus Christ is Lord and that He died on the cross to break the barrier of sin separating mankind from God the Father. Further, by His death, Jesus opened the way for believers to live under God's grace by our faith in Jesus' wonderful gift to mankind. Specifically, accessing that grace stems from our faith in Him, His deity, His magnificent sacrifice, and the power and glory of God's love upon us, daily and always.

Tithing in the New Testament age provides a believer the ability to access one of God's all-time great promises (Malachi 3:10) and to glorify God while advancing the kingdom. God provides us with unlimited grace in this age, and you access that grace by faith. Accessing that grace by faith in His promises (including tithing) is still a wonderful way to please God.

If you feel called upon to explore this approach to God's grace, then let's get started!

Tithing In The Old Testament

What Is Tithing & Why Should You Tithe?

A tithe is 10% of your income or increase that you give first, upon receipt, before any other spending, to your local church. "A tenth of the produce of the land, whether grain or fruit, is the Lord's, and is holy" (Leviticus 27:30 TLB). A tithe is a 10% portion of your resources given as an offering to your local church. Other money to missions, crusades, or good causes outside the local church are offerings.

In Hebrew, "tithe" means tenth. Tithing is practiced by both Jews and Christians as a doctrine of faith, but tithing itself is largely mentioned only in the Old Testament.

1. You tithe on your increase in whatever form. For example, you tithe of your land and what grows on it. "A tithe of everything from the land, whether grain from the soil or fruit from the trees, belongs to the LORD; it is holy to the LORD" (Leviticus 27:30).

2. You tithe of the cattle and livestock that graze upon the land. "Every tithe of the herd and flock—every tenth animal that passes under the shepherd's rod—will be holy to the Lord" (Leviticus 27:32).

3. You tithe of the increase you experience through God's blessings. The above was written in the time of an agrarian society when people counted increase by foals rather than return on investments. Still, the principle applies to both livestock and stocks and bonds.

We will go into this in more detail later but consider this: "Honor the Lord with your wealth, with the firstfruits of all your crops; then your barns will be filled to overflowing, and your vats will brim over with new wine" (Proverbs 3:9–10). That is a great promise that lives on today even in the New Testament age. Believe in the power that works inside of you.

How Do You Figure the Tithe?

Imagine you are a tradesman with skill in carpentry. You are asked to build an upstairs, outdoor patio for a client overlooking a distant lake. You take three trips out to the site: one to meet with the client and contract for the job, the second to oversee the delivery of the lumber and metal work, the last for you and your helpers to build the patio. Your gas and mileage, your payment for the costs of construction, the cost of labor, and the two nights of lodging for you and your workers amounts to $15,000. You charge $30,000 for the entire project.

What is your increase? The net is $15,000 to you as profit or increase. What should your tithe be? $1,500 or 1/10th of your increase.

This is a simple approach and leaves out the issue of taxes. Where do taxes figure in the analysis? I think this is an issue of the heart for the believer who wants to tithe, but for me, I would rely on what Jesus said in Matthew 22:21: "Therefore render to Caesar the things that are Caesar's, and to God the things that are God's" (ESV).

Jesus made a distinction between two kingdoms. There is a kingdom of this world where Caesar holds power and another kingdom not of this world where Jesus is King. Christians are part of both kingdoms while here on Earth. Under Caesar, we have certain obligations where we presently live involving material things. Under Christ, we have other obligations involving eternal things. If Caesar demands money, give it to him. But make sure you also give God what gives you peace and joy. For me and many others, joy shows up in tithing.

So, for me, I would deduct the taxes in determining my net increase if I knew the amount of the tax. I would pay the tithe in full without the deduction if I did not find peace in the first approach. Praying for personal guidance as to how to proceed on this matter and finding peace through the Holy Spirit is key. Giving a little more to make sure you have peace in the matter never hurts.

It is a matter of the heart. Let your spirit be your umpire.

Consider These Aspects to Tithing

It is not your money you are tithing, but God's money because God owns it all:

- "The earth is the Lord's, and everything in it, the world, and all who live in it" (Psalm 24:1).

- "The whole earth is mine" (Exodus 19:5).

- "To the Lord your God belong the heavens, even the highest heavens, the earth and everything in it" (Deuteronomy 10:14).

- "For in him all things were created: things in heaven and on earth, visible and invisible, whether thrones or powers or rulers or authorities; all things have been created through him and for him" (Colossians 1:16).

Why Tithe?

God created mankind for several reasons that will be discussed later in this book. For now, think of it this way: In the garden, Adam and Eve depended upon God for everything. Then, they sinned by eating the forbidden fruit. Sin broke the relationship with God because God could have nothing to do with the imperfect. Still, because of God's love, He wanted a relationsip with humankind. Starting with the gifts of Cain and Abel (where Abel's gift was accepted but Cain's was not), down to Abraham and Melchizedek (an archetype of the preincarnate Jesus), to the creation of the nation of Israel, and on to when Christ lived as a human on Earth, God has longed to get His people to rely on Him.

Giving firstfruits, both in this age and in the time before Christ, honoring God with our firstfruits has been a way to show our dependence on Him. It is that relationship God longs for and why God blesses those who rely on Him in faith.

God loves your faith, loves when you turn to Him as your loving Father who wants only the best for you! It's faith that moves Him, not your money. The money you give is a way of communicating your faith. Giving to God first before taking care of other needs or demands on your funds shows you are honoring Him and relying on Him to honor that faith.

Giving a tenth from your firstfruits demonstrates your faith that He will take care of you. He loves us to depend on Him. Tithing tangibly demonstrates that.

Are There Other Reasons to Tithe?

Tithing shows that you trust God and rely on Him in faith. If God really owns everything, then He doesn't need your money. You need to tithe for your benefit.

- Tithing shows God that we trust Him with our lives and our finances.

- Tithing reminds us to rely on God to meet our needs.

- It makes us more aware of the needs of others too.

- Our tithing supports our pastors and the local church.

- Tithing helps your local church actively be the church by helping others.

- Tithing encourages a grateful and generous spirit.

- Tithing can help steer us away from being greedy or loving money too much.

- Being outrageously generous is a blast!

Do I Have to Tithe?

In the Old Testament, the answer was yes, you had to tithe. In fact, as we will see, the Israelites had to give more than 10% on various occasions. The reason for tithing was that the tithe was partly for the civil government of the nation and partly for the support of the priests and religious administration. Christians are largely living in nations, such as the United States, that require taxes separate from the support of a particular religion. We don't pay tithes to our governing bodies.

The standard of New Testament giving was described by Paul in 2 Corinthians 9:7 "not grudgingly, or of necessity: for God loveth a cheerful giver" (KJV). Why the different standards? The Law was onerous, and compliance was hard. It was intentionally difficult to show the Old Testament Israelites their need for a savior. No man could comply with the standards of the Law every time, every day.

Now, we have a Savior. We do not live under the Law but under God's grace—unmerited favor obtained by believing in Jesus and His saving work on the cross. That said, moral laws still apply. We should honor our God and our parents. We should not steal, kill, or lie. We should honor our neighbors by not coveting or committing adultery. These laws are still beneficial to us and our society.

So too with tithing.

It also doesn't mean you're a bad Christian if you don't tithe. It does mean you are missing out. Why do I say that? Because the promises of Malachi 3:10 have never been repealed. Indeed, God says in Malachi 3:6: "For I am the LORD, I change not" (KJV).

You are missing out on something spectacular if you do not tithe.

How Should I Increase My Giving When I Start Making More Money?

First, when you start tithing, expect God to surprise you with blessings from unexpected sources. God promises blessings in all forms in Malachi 3:10. In fact, when you are starting to tithe, why don't you read that verse every day? Depending on God is the essence of faith, and God loves to reward faith in every form. Fortunately, tithing is a great way to keep a record of your faith in Him.

That should not change when you make more money. The tenth is a great percentage to measure against for your giving, and giving is a great way to live!

Also, when money comes in, think of it as a great opportunity to give above and beyond your tithe. Many regular tithers often give well above 10%.

Action Step: Write out Malachi 3:10 and place it somewhere you will see it every day.

Not Grudgingly Nor of Necessity

Do not get involved in foolish discussions about spiritual pedigrees or in quarrels and fights about obedience to Jewish laws. These things are useless and a waste of time.

— Titus 3:9 NLT

So let each one give as he purposes in his heart, not grudgingly nor of necessity; for God loves a cheerful giver.

—2 Corinthians 9:7 NKJV

With this book, I am not seeking to impose an outdated rule on your giving. We live in the age of grace (thank God!), and the laws of the Old Testament have been replaced with the vibrancy of an active relationship with God the Father through faith in Jesus Christ, our Lord. Further, we are blessed with the Holy Spirit living inside of us, providing guidance as to how to live our lives daily and second by second if we let Him. Our focus on sin as the barrier between God and man is gone! Now, God is no longer stymied by our imperfections in blessing us. Now, because of Jesus' grace, we can have an ongoing, vibrant relationship with God that has unlimited potential for our blessings through Him and through our faith, as we daily align ourselves more towards God's character and the guidance of the Holy Spirit. Praise God!

I am not trying to enforce obedience to Jewish laws; I am trying to communicate that God loves and rewards our faith. In the Old Testament, God gave the Jews a requirement: tithing. Tithe as described by the Old Testament and you will be blessed. Don't tithe and you will miss out on blessings. To encourage His people after their return to the Promised Land, God made a promise in Malachi 3:10 that relates to tithing and has never been revoked. Because it hasn't been revoked, the blessings it provides are still available to you.

You, however, in the New Testament age, are not compelled to tithe. For you, it is a free option, still backed by the Malachi 3:10 promise that offers a guarantee of exorbitant blessings.

Why should you act now? Yes, I know this sounds like a late-night TV commercial. But, giving of your hard-earned money at a 10% clip requires an extreme attention to God with a heart leaning into Him greatly. What parents don't like when their child, full of faith in the parent, acts in accordance with the parent's wishes? Consider the parent's happiness when the ask is something big, like giving away a cherished toy, while trusting the parent's love and wisdom in the action that everything will work out for the best.

That's why God loves a cheerful giver and continues to honor an Old Testament promise into the new church age. He loves it when you evidence, even monetize, your faith in Him.

Are you required to take advantage of what God says about tithing? No, your relationship with God is to be active, interactive, and full of faith in Him to take full advantage of His grace. Accessing His grace by faith is how New Testament believers interact with God now, not the Law. In fact, tithing predates the Law.

If tithing predates the Law, and we are not under the Law, should we no longer practice tithing? Not necessarily. As Jesus said during his incarnation, "You should tithe, yes, but you should not leave these other things undone" (Luke 11:42 TLB). While he was busy fulfilling the Law when he said this, he never intimated that tithing was something that should disappear with the Old Testament age.

Still, as we will discuss when we get to Malachi 3:10, God has shown us the depth of His care and desire to bless us in that verse. Tithing was and is a pathway to pleasing Him. It provides an insight into His desires for us. And it is a promise, one He tells us, "I the Lord do not change" (Malachi 3:6).

This discussion should not end without specifically addressing scams and a "this for that" approach to giving. Think of the woman who gave the two mites, of whom Jesus said she had given more than anyone (Mark 12:41–44 and Luke 21:1–4). God looks to the heart in our giving. Giving involves a leap of faith that requires us to release something tangible in faith to communicate our love and confidence in Him. That faith, communicated by giving, glorifies Him in that He knows you trust Him and His love for you.

Giving in a sense of "Hey God, I gave a hundred bucks, now you owe me a car" will get you nowhere. I know. I have tried, as will be discussed later. As with most things in our relationship with God, He wants to see you trust that He loves you and that He wants only the best for you. Give, not grudgingly or of necessity, but cheerfully in faith and trust that He knows what's best.

You are not commanded to tithe. Still, since God's promise to bless tithing has never been abrogated, it is easy and logical to believe that He will still honor His word.

And it is a really good promise!!!!

Points To Consider:

Do you tithe on gifts you receive?

Do you tithe on loans you incur?

Do you tithe on dividends or profits made on investments?

What constitutes "increase"?

Why should I tithe? It is no longer a requirement for believers. In fact, it never was a requirement for Christians but only for Jews living under the Law, so why should I do this?

Our Story

Bring the whole tithe into the storehouse, that there may be food in my house. Test me in this," says the Lord *Almighty, "and see if I will not throw open the floodgates of heaven and pour out so much blessing that there will not be room enough to store it.*

—Malachi 3:10

My wife, Carol, and I started tithing due to a personal crisis. At the end of 1995, my job as a federal employee was eliminated. My wife and three kids (all under the age of eight) had been living comfortably on our double income with a nice house and enough money to at least break even every month.

But we had debt, a big mortgage and suddenly half our income disappeared. We sat down and took an inventory, did some forecasting, and realized we were not going to make it if we didn't start tithing.

What? We were running out of money, so we needed to give more money? Exactly, only with a twist: think of Matthew 14:15–21:

> As evening approached, the disciples came to him and said, "This is a remote place, and it's already getting late. Send the crowds away, so they can go to the villages and buy themselves some food."
>
> Jesus replied, "They do not need to go away. You give them something to eat."
>
> "We have here only five loaves of bread and two fish," they answered.
>
> "Bring them here to me," he said. And he directed the people to sit down on the grass. Taking the five loaves and the two fish and looking up to heaven, he gave thanks and broke the loaves. Then he gave them to the disciples, and the disciples gave them to the people. They all ate and were satisfied, and the disciples picked up twelve basketfuls of broken pieces that were left over. The number of those who ate was about five thousand men, besides women and children.

That was quite a miracle. The miracle occurred because Jesus got involved in the process; they had five loaves and two fish, but by first putting the fish and loaves in Jesus' hands, they fed the 5,000 and had 12 bushels left over. That is basically how tithing works—firstfruits to Him by faith and outstanding blessings back to you.

That was what we were doing with our tithe, the tithe that God had promised to bless in Malachi 3:10. We had been going to church fitfully before the kids were born and sporadically attended and gave since. Now, things were serious.

We prayed about it and decided to give the first of our money to our church—10% of our income/increase in whatever form. Any other giving, to good causes or other ministries, was to be over that amount. We took a deep breath and got started.

We gave as she was paid twice a month. Surprisingly, in January 1996, we received an amount equal to our giving, almost to the penny, from an unexpected source.

For the next eight months, we gave, and divinely, money equal to our giving came back to us. This was not just a happenstance. This was supernatural.

Do you want to experience joy? Watch God deliver when you fully depend on Him. We were at that place and every month it got easier to rely on Him.

I compare this to a child standing on a diving board with the parents in the pool, urging the child to jump. The child looks at the circumstances of being on a board over water and wonders if the parent will make good on catching them, despite the parent continuing to say "Come on! Jump! I'll catch you!"

Finally, the child jumps, the parent catches the child, and you see the child light up with joy! They immediately want to do it again. And again. And it becomes all they want to do for the rest of the afternoon.

Tithing is like that. Seeing God bless your faith in Him by working supernaturally in your finances has been one of the great blessings of our lives. Tithing is one of my favorite joys of the last 30 years.

In September of that year, we gave, and no money flowed back to us. Rather, our two oldest children were cited in school for some honors. I wish I had written it down at that time. What I distinctly remember is my saying at the time: "This is better than money!"

God's blessings are not just financial. They are blessings in all aspects of your life.

In October 1996, the money flow returned. I am not making this up: we would give, and God returned an amount equal to the gift every month (except that September). It was sometimes to the penny but never more than five dollars from what we gave and usually a little more.

November came and then came Christmas, a time to spend extravagantly and beyond our means on our credit cards, as has become our nation's tradition.

Christmas was wonderful but then came January.

By now, I had a one-man business originating apartment loans for an FHA Lender in San Francisco. My job was to contact developers and apartment owners to interest them in pursuing an FHA loan. Perhaps you didn't know, but about 95% of FHA's business is 1–4-unit properties, which are considered "single family" but duplexes, triplexes, and quadruplexes fall into this category as well. Around four percent of FHA's business is in multifamily properties—five units or more—which include affordable/low-income properties, conversion of office buildings into housing, and some of the nicest high-end apartment properties to be found, including in Plano and other high-end cities. The remaining 1% or so includes hospitals and other properties that include an element of housing.

I was receiving a small draw to generate apartment loans for the firm. The draw I was receiving went entirely to office expenses each month, and I still had not actually made any money. Carol remained the breadwinner.

In the second week of January 1997, seemingly all on the same day, the bills came for all three of our major credit cards. Tentatively, we opened each one. Almost exactly, they said the same thing: "Because of your good credit, you do not need to make a payment this month."

How does that happen? It might have been a national program followed by each company, but to us, it was God's deliverance! Once again, God supernaturally had our back.

From there, things got easier. Soon after, I closed a loan and finally made some money. We tithed. My career as an apartment lender began to accelerate with more loans, which led to me getting a job as regional vice president at the firm that was the largest FHA apartment lender at the time. Do not miss the supernatural acceleration of my employment, from working in a windowless, one-man office between the restrooms and the break room of an executive suite, to being a regional VP in the biggest company in my field, all of which was provided by God.

This led us to start our own firm in 2008, a horrible year for real estate finance of any kind, but God led the way. Part of God's leading took the form of me enrolling in "The Master's Program" (now called "Priority Living"), a California-based, non-denominational, Christian organization with a lot of young and middle-aged business executives seeking a life of significance to add to their success. Our path led adventurously and eventually to a profitable firm that we sold in 2023.

This was an Ephesians 3:20 event: "Now unto him that is able to do exceeding abundantly above all that we ask or think, according to the power that worketh in us" (KJV). I directly trace all this financial success to God's provision, honoring our commitment to Him and our tithe. Our road has had some intense drama over the years; still, not once has God disappointed us. Believing in Him has gotten so much easier, and the blessings continue to grow.

Our story so far suggests economic blessing because we relied on tithing. Because tithing requires faith in God's word and God rewards faith, we have been richly blessed in many aspects of our marriage and with our family. God has blessed us greatly; He has also tested us greatly, in part, to sharpen our awareness of His presence in our lives and the need for us to lean into Him during times of trials. Let me explain.

Mortgage bankers sell money. What is unique to real estate financing of any kind is that you have no control over the product you are selling. Chickens get sick in China, somebody runs a ship into a busy passageway to a port, a bank lends too much on crypto and fails, and then, rates go up. As a small mortgage company, you have no control over any of a thousand things that can daily impact the rates you can charge. When rates break in your favor, it's great. When the market turns against you, things can get really ugly, really fast; a small interest rate change can impact a loan by several hundred thousand dollars or more to the good or bad.

As you can imagine, over 30 years of tithing and forty-plus years of being in this business, we have experienced a lot of intense drama, in part because the numbers for construction of a 250-unit apartment property run into tens of millions of dollars. Rightly or wrongly, people tend to blame the lender who is selling a product it can't control if expectations are not met. There have been many sleepless nights, some interspersed with ugly cries and all involving intense prayers and reading of the Bible (I strongly endorse Psalm 51 and Psalm 91 for such occasions). Looking back, none of these ugly situations turned out as badly as I thought and many ended miraculously with only God's intervention keeping us from crushing financial losses.

Now, I look back and see God's hand in allowing it and Him strengthening me and our relationship. As discussed later, the 23rd Psalm says "yea, though I walk through the valley of the shadow of death, I will fear no evil: for thou art with me; thy rod and thy staff, they comfort me" (Psalm 23:4 KJV). God rarely takes opposition, unfair circumstances, or dramatic crises away from us. He is, however, right there to help, ever present in times of need.

Over the years, I have seen this situation play out enough times to know quickly who can wipe these tears, provide comfort, and put things on the mend when I lean into Him. Now, while I might go astray for a short while, I know to quickly turn to the Lord.

I heard a preacher once say: The Bible tells us in the end, "all is well." If everything goes wrong, I am still to regain my peace. Sometimes, often in fact, it is great to sit quietly, praying as you watch, to see how He is going to settle it. His way is the best, and I can testify to that.

Points To Consider:

Tithing is an Old Testament requirement. Why should I rely on a requirement Christ has already fulfilled?

Am I required to tithe in the New Testament age?

Am I disappointing God if I don't tithe?

Am I disappointing God if I give to other places besides the local church?

Does the promise of Malachi 3:10 still apply, or was it only an Old Testament promise?

Think of this: God loves you, whatever you do. God has made you a promise about tithing: do it and He promises blessings. Will it always be financial blessing? I don't know. It hasn't always been financial in my experience.

What is important to God—who doesn't need your money—is you stepping out in faith and trusting Him. Here is a blueprint for blessing, perhaps financial but maybe not. I do know Ephesians 3:20 is also promised.

He doesn't want your money; He wants your heart, your faith in Him. God loves your faith in relying on Him. Your tithe communicates your faith. If you give tithe, acting in faith, you will be rewarded. His promise is still valid in the New Testament age.

Old Testament Tithing

Before the Law

Giving is first recognized in the Bible with Cain and Abel. The result, as you will see, was mixed and kind of depressing.

Almost 2,000 years later, God selected Abram (soon to be Abraham) to be the father of His chosen people. Abraham fathered a son of his self-effort, Ishmael, which thwarted direct communication between God and Abraham for 13 years. At that time, Sarai became Sarah, got pregnant, and Isaac, the chosen one, the chosen line, was born.

The story of Abraham and tithing, Isaac and tithing, and Jacob and tithing are told over nearly two hundred years. Then, we have Egypt and eventually, Moses and the Law, and the codification of tithing into Jewish law.

Following this is a long descent by the Jews that leads to the last book of the Old Testament by the prophet, Malachi. Malachi (circa 430 BC) is the most important writer on the subject of tithing, and when he finished, God did not speak to His people for over 400 years, until around 30 AD when John the Baptist began to preach.

The fact that tithing predates the codification of the Law suggests that tithing was not a product of the Law, but for its operative time, the Law included tithing. It is also appropriate to explain that tithing remains now not because of Jewish law but as a continuing method to honor, worship, and revere God with the belief it is pleasing to Him.

This is not legalism but a form of worship that God has always approved and continues to approve. It is a form of showing our awesome God our heartfelt appreciation for His place in our lives and all He does for us, daily and throughout our lifetimes.

Among other things, the giving of money from our increase shows we recognize from where all blessings originate. Not me, Lord, but thee.

Points To Consider:

What are the elements of tithing?

Income and Increase; 10% of the income or increase and giving to the local church.

Was the Mosaic Law the start of tithing?

No, tithing started perhaps 2,500 years before the Law. Certainly, Abram gave 10% around 450 years before the Law.

Is tithing required now?

No. The Old Testament laws are no longer the standard of our life with God. Christ changed that relationship by his sacrifice on the cross.

Look at Numbers 7, which discusses the offerings at the dedication of the Tabernacle. Each tribe brought the very same offerings to God as they dedicated their place of worship. Why did God include in the scriptures the very same list 12 times?

I think it was because He was pleased and wanted to recognize individually the gifts of each tribe. He honored each tribe's dedication in Numbers 7. He will honor any gift you give from the heart (not grudgingly nor of necessity). What He says about tithing is specific to that form of giving and it still applies today.

**God loves it when you give
in a heartfelt manner.**

Unforced Rhythms of Grace

Look, I am a New Testament believer too. I think living in the Old Testament age would have been exhausting. I like Jesus' unforced rhythms of grace: "Are you tired? Worn out? Burned out on religion? Come to me. Get away with me and you'll recover your life. I'll show you how to take a real rest. Walk with me and work with me—watch how I do it. Learn the unforced rhythms of grace. I won't lay anything heavy or ill-fitting on you. Keep company with me and you'll learn to live freely and lightly" (Matthew 11:28–30 MSG).

Unforced rhythms of grace—yeah, that is more my style. But what does that mean?

The Old Testament was transactional: do good and get good. The New Testament is relational, based on the finished works of Christ on the cross. Tithing in the New Testament can become a mix of these two methods of interacting with God. Don't do that. If you think your efforts in tithing in the New Testament Age deserve a payback for what you have done or are doing, don't tithe. Your efforts are nothing compared to the cross.

Instead, consider this: tithing in the New Testament is a way to thank God and recognize His magnificence and His magnificent gift of Jesus. You give from adoration, from love, and as worship. You don't give from an expectation of benefit.

It communicates recognition of His majesty and place in your life—think of Abraham being so overwhelmed by God's glory that he gave a tenth of his spoils from victory to Melchizedek. Your tithe in the New Testament age is relational, not demanded. You know your friend, your God. You know all He has done for you.

He no longer demands a tithe but He has always liked the tithe, even before it became the Law for the Jews. God does not change and He still likes the tithe, if given in the right spirit, not grudgingly nor of necessity but cheerfully.

You tithe in the New Testament because you know your friend, your God. He is the one you walk with and converse with daily. He has always liked the tithe even though it is no longer demanded as a law.

New Testament tithing is a blessing given to God, done with a heart of confidence in and adoration of Him. We know He will work out every situation if we trust Him.

He has always liked the tithe and I want to please Him, not as an obligation but as a friend who recognizes His first place in my life and the blessings the priority has given me and continues to give me daily. I want to live my life fully aligned with Him, His thoughts and His blessings.

A REALLY QUICK OLD TESTAMENT OVERVIEW

God created a perfect world and gave its dominion to Adam and Eve. Satan conned them and stole the dominion of Earth from mankind, who pretty much stumbled around for thousands of years, constantly disappointing God.

Adam and Eve were expelled from the Garden. Their two sons, Cain and Abel, gave the first recorded gifts to God. God accepted Abel's gift but not Cain's. Cain slew Abel.

Many generations of humankind lived for centuries until God found a man after His own heart in Abraham and used his line to be God's chosen people. The promised child was Abraham's son, Isaac.

A lot happened to Isaac and his son Jacob, culminating in Jacob's family of 69 moving to Egypt, and after a while, they were held in Egypt for 430 years, most of that time in slavery. They were there long enough to develop a slave mentality.

God chose Moses to lead them out of slavery after some severely strong miracles convinced Pharoah to let them go. Pharoah changed his mind and went after the Israelites at the Red Sea. God parted the Red Sea for the Israelites to cross on dry land.

I like how it has been described as a birth passage for the Israelites, changing a family that started as 69 people into a nation of around 2,000,000 people upon their delivery across the Red Sea. Then, God began the process of turning this nation into His people, the people to be charged with witnessing to the world and rectifying the loss launched by the garden fiasco.

God told them if they obeyed His laws, they would be blessed. The people, somewhat casually, somewhat arrogantly, said: Oh yeah, we can surely do everything you ask us to do (Exodus 19:8). Every time any person—that's you and me—uses human effort over God's grace, things get difficult.

I picture a moment of incredulity on God's part. You can surely do what? You have whined and disobeyed ever since you left Egypt. You can't feed yourselves, and you whine about the food. You break every rule I give you, and now, you are saying you can do everything I ask you to do? We'll see.

He then gave them the Ten Commandments, which proved they could not comply with the Law and demonstrated the need for a savior. When He shared these laws with so many of the rules ending with "or you will die," He does not sound pleased.

The Savior came, Jesus Christ. He completed the Law and gave us a new way of relating to God as His children, not His servants. Think of it this way: Old Testament believers served God. We now are able to live in a right relationship with God. In essence, God now serves us, allowing us to live freely and joyfully in right relationship with Him.

Jesus was born and lived as a Jew and as the perfect Lamb of God. Jesus eliminated the sin barrier separating God and humankind. Sin was dealt with on the cross, and Jesus' death satisfied God's perfect justice. His resurrection then bridged the chasm between God and humankind.

Now, when God looks at a believer, He does not see a sinner. He sees someone who has accepted His gift of the perfect lamb, our Savior Jesus. Sin is no longer the dividing issue. The light we carry with the indwelling of the Holy Spirit identifies us as one of His own.

This is a decision to accept Christ as our Savior, made in faith. As we will be reminded throughout this book, faith in God the Father and the precious gift of His Son is the key to everything in your life.

The indwelling of the Holy Spirit, God in us, longs to guide you on the right path daily, to prompt you to action, to warn you of pitfalls and wrong decisions, and to generally promote your relationship with Jesus and God's love for you. This is the path to fullness in life, a long successful life led by the Holy Spirit.

Don't ignore those promptings. Marvelous things can happen (and terrible things can be avoided) if you are sensitive to the insights the Holy Spirit is providing you. Become acquainted with the process of hearing from God inside you—the Holy Spirit who is the administrator for the new covenant God the Father has provided through His Son. Allow the Holy Spirit to renew you (Titus 3:5). Trust Him. Pray and listen for the voice of direction, warning, comfort, and joy.

The Ten Commandments were turned into 613 laws by the Israelites to legislate morality and obedience to God. It failed for many reasons and proved that human self-effort could not keep the laws of God. It wasn't in their hearts.

Points To Consider:

Christ died for all and wiped away sin as a barrier to relationship between God and humankind (reflect on this sentence for a moment).

The sacrifice of Jesus on the cross eliminated sin as an issue between God and humankind. When God looks at a believer, He doesn't see a sinner, but He sees the light of a believer in Jesus.

His son, His sacrifice. Sin is no longer the issue (see Romans 6:11; Galatians 5:18; 1 John 3:20; Romans 8:9–10).

God's grace is now preeminent in our relationship. Sin is not the issue for believers: "For I will be merciful to their unrighteousness, and their sins and their iniquities will I remember no more" Hebrews 8:12 KJV). Think of that! God does not remember our sins!

In the church age, a lot of the relationship between God and humankind has changed, but God's promise of blessing in tithing remains.

TITHING BEFORE THE LAW

Cain and Abel

The first thing to note here is that giving goes all the way back to Cain and Abel, and it likely involved giving a tenth (though I can't prove that). The Old Testament before the Law of Moses mentions giving in three places including two specific instances of tithing.

Cain and Abel are the first givers in the Bible. Ten percent is not mentioned as the standard but certainly God expected firstfruits. Indeed, Cain's failure to give his firstfruits denied God the ability to bless him because of Cain's lack of faith. He lost blessings even though he gave because it was not the first of his increase. This incident led Cain down a path to murder his brother, Abel, and resulted in a dreadful, nomadic life with a scar on his forehead identifying him as the original murderer. Certainly, Cain's actions demonstrate the need to give from firstfruits, as giving firstfruits demonstrates faith in God, the only way in which anyone can please Him.

Did God need his firstfruits? No, God owns everything and that included Cain's produce. Then what was the big deal? God wanted Cain's heart, his faith in God, and his appreciation of everything God had done and was doing on behalf of His sons. Cain's heart is the "heart of the matter." He doubted God would take care of him and only came forward with a gift when he knew he had more stashed for his own provision. There is no glory to God in such an approach. God loves it when you exhibit faith in Him.

Cain and Abel and the Principle of Firstfruits

Let's look deeper into why God accepted Abel's gift and not Cain's.

Now Abel kept flocks, and Cain worked the soil. *In the course of time* [emphasis added] Cain brought some of the fruits of the soil as an offering to the Lord. And Abel also brought an offering—fat portions from some of the *firstborn* [emphasis added] of his flock. The Lord looked with favor on Abel and his offering, but on Cain and his offering he did not look with favor. So, Cain was very angry and his face was downcast.

Then the Lord said to Cain, "Why are you angry? Why is your face downcast? If you do what is right, will you not be accepted? But if you do not do what is right, sin is crouching at your door; it desires to have you, but you must rule over it" (Genesis 4:2-7).

The answer, at least in part, is that Abel gave from the firstfruits of his toil, showing God that he relied on God to provide for his needs after giving the gift. His faith was demonstrated by relying on God because he did not know for sure when he gave that there would be any more additions to his flock. He exhibited faith in God to provide. Cain did not give from his firstfruits but waited to make sure he had enough, and then he gave to God. Between the two of them, Abel exhibited faith in God by giving without the tangible assurance of any return. That return would be received due to faithful reliance on God. Cain missed that point, and his life went downhill because of it.

Tithing with the firstfruits means you, in your capacity, have no certainty that anything more will be forthcoming. You are showing God that you trust Him more than the weather, more than your livestock, more than the stock market, and more than your own abilities. You are relying on Him by faith, and He loves and rewards that.

Let's look at faith in God in another context: Say you are a child who comes to your father saying "Dad, I know I don't deserve it, and I know you probably are busy and probably won't do what I ask, but if it isn't too much trouble, could I have a dollar?" If the dad gives the child the dollar, where is the spark, the feeling of satisfaction for the father that his child trusts him to make good on his love for his child? That approach, the mealy-mouth request, does not honor the Father. There is no joy for God in such an approach; rather, "let us then approach God's throne of grace with confidence, so that we may receive mercy and find grace to help us in our time of need" (Hebrews 4:16).

This embodies the type of faith God wants us to exhibit when we approach Him. In your life, give with confidence. Tithing is about the clearest approach to show God you are focused on Him and His provision. We should give freely (okay, tithe), make bold requests, and rest at peace, knowing God wants to fulfill (or exceed in His own manner) those requests made in faith and to share in your joy when you receive. Bold requests made in faith make God happy!

It is the same spark that happens in tithing when you give from the firstfruits not knowing what will follow. But you give, knowing that it is God's good pleasure to bless your tithe, "exceedingly abundantly above all that we ask or think, according to the power that works in us" (Ephesians 3:20 NKJV).

That power that works inside of us is faith, and it takes faith to tithe, but wow! The blessings are more than you could ask or think!

Firstfruits

Tithe, the sacrifice of the firstborn, and the giving of the firstfruits predate the Levitical Law in practice and remain today, despite the succession of the Law into grace. That grace is Jesus, full of grace and truth (John 1:14). But one cannot say that the moral laws of the commandments have been superseded by the New Testament. Murder, lying, dishonoring parents, coveting, adultery, stealing, and unjust weights and measures are still intrinsically wrong. God instituted tithing as a supernatural way to bless those who, by faith, depend on Him to deliver on His promise. God longs to fulfill the promises of Malachi 3:10 just as much now as He did in ancient times; He does not change.

The tithe belongs to God, and the firstfruits belong to God. He promises blessings to those who honor Him by following this approach to living.

Why Does Tithe Have to be First?

To comply with God's intent for tithing, the tithe must be first. God must be first in your life for all the blessings He promises you to be fully operational in your life. Exodus 20:2–3 says, "I am the Lord your God, who brought you out of Egypt, out of the land of slavery. You shall have no other gods before me." God will not be second place in your life. He is first, higher than all, before all, the way, the truth, and the life (John 14:6).

If you are giving money to God, it is His New-Testament-age desire that it be the first funds that will be blessed. I am not saying that He will not bless funds that are not firstfruits in the present age, but I know He blesses people according to the terms of Malachi 3:10 even now. Keeping the order of tithe remains important for blessing.

In the Old Testament, tithing was demanded. Why? Because it is His nature to be first, to be preeminent. He cannot deny His nature or essence. That is why God accepted Abel's gift and not Cain's in the first record of gifts to God. Even God has limits: God cannot do anything that contradicts the essence of who He is.

Would you really want a God who could tolerate the imperfect, who graded on a curve and let even the tiniest detail slide? NO! God's inability to associate with any sinful imperfection led to Melchizedek meeting with Abraham ("for all have sinned and fall short of the glory of God" (Romans 3:23)), and ultimately, Jesus coming in human form to fulfill the bridge from God to humankind.

By honoring the Lord "with your wealth, with the firstfruits of all your crops, then your barns will be filled to overflowing, and your vats will brim over with new wine" (Proverbs 3:9–10). "No one is to appear before me empty-handed" (Exodus 23:15). The tithe recognized God's provision. The firstfruits recognized the quality of the provision.

The children saw the parents give systematically according to God's word. Honoring God in this way was passed down through generations from the richest to the poorest families.

God promises blessings to those who honor Him. Tithe, ten percent of your income and increase, paid first from your money, promises the most excellent supernatural blessings—overflowing and brimming over blessings.

Don't knock it if you haven't tried it. It is a promise from God that still stands.

He is perfect and cannot tolerate or be part of any kind of imperfection. Thank you, Jesus, for bridging the gap between God the Father and us sinners, who are considered as saints with our belief in your saving work on the cross!

Points To Consider:

Why did God demand the firstfruits of our increase?

Why is it right for us to obey this requirement?

What is the key element to giving first fruit for you to be blessed?

How did Cain's gift differ from Abel's?

Why was that difference key to God's response?

What happened to Cain when He didn't follow God's plan?

Does this suggest God took tithing seriously?

Where was faith in God exhibited between Cain and Abel?

God is not second in anything. You might treat Him as such, and if you do and confess, He will forgive you, perhaps without penalty or loss of blessing if that is what He determines. But a moment for a full blessing might have been missed. Don't get legalistic with this comment— God is amazing grace and His Son died on the cross to open this channel between us. But still, realize who you are dealing with.

The Patriarchal Period

Noah

Noah was the tenth generation from Adam and the grandson of Methuselah, who was the oldest man to ever live. Culminating with the lifetime of Noah, humanity had gotten off track in many ways. The worst was that demonic angels were having relations with human women. Why was this a problem? Because God had promised "And I will put enmity between you and the woman, and between your offspring and *hers* [emphasis added]; he will crush your head, and you will strike his heel" (Genesis 3:15). The problem was that if Satan's angels were able to continue impregnating the women of mankind, there would be no true humanity left to fulfill the prophecy.

There were other reasons for the flood, and the fact that there was one true believer in God available to build the Ark over 120 years is a testament to God's discernment and Noah's obedience. Still, for our purposes, the important place to focus is:

Then Noah built an altar to the Lord and, taking some of all the clean animals and clean birds, he sacrificed burnt offerings on it. The Lord smelled the pleasing aroma and said in his heart: "Never again will I curse the ground because of humans, even though every inclination of the human heart is evil from childhood. And never again will I destroy all living creatures, as I have done.

"As long as the earth endures, seedtime and harvest, cold and heat, summer and winter, day and night will never cease" (Genesis 8:20–22).

After 120 years of building the Ark under constant harassment from his neighbors, let alone the monumental task of building a nearly 500-foot ship capable of storing two (or more in some cases) of all the animals and their different foods, Noah then spent six months of confinement on the Ark waiting for the earth to dry. When he got out of the Ark, he first honored God with a sacrifice, acknowledging the creator. This faith and obedience were honored by God and has served as a blessing for every generation since. The success of his task also led to the continuance of true humanity, leading to Jesus and to our salvation. God has blessed us through Noah and Noah blessed us with his gift to God.

Noah endured 120 years of harassment and ridicule, not to mention hard work. How do you think faith kept him going? The whole world was flooded except for him and his family. He was entrusted with the charge of repopulating the world.

In the end, God rewarded Noah with being the father of the last remaining strand of true humanity.

Points To consider:

Did he have reasons to trust the Lord? Was he blessed for his following God all those years?

What is the key element in his survival and later thriving?

Abraham, Isaac, and Jacob

The first mention of tithe as ten percent comes with the story of Abraham around 2,000 years after Cain and Abel. The story of the life of Abraham, as told in Genesis, starts with Abraham being called by God to leave the house of his father, Terah, and to settle in the land of Canaan. God promises this land to Abraham and his descendants, hence "The Promised Land."

This promise is subsequently inherited by *Isaac*, Abraham's son by his wife *Sarah*. His birth can only be described as miraculous and came from Abraham and Sarah's belief that God could provide a child to them even in their old age (Isaac, the son of the promise, was born to them when Abraham was one hundred years old, while Sarah was 90 years old). Isaac's half-brother, *Ishmael,* is also promised to be the founder of a great nation.

Sarah died. Abraham purchased a tomb (the *Cave of the Patriarchs*) at *Hebron* to be Sarah's grave, thus establishing his right to the land. In the second generation, Isaac marries Rebekah with his parents' approval. And so, the story towards the promised child proceeds.

Abraham and Melchizedek (Part 1)

Abraham lived around 1900 BC. He grew up in the Ur of Chaldees (modern day Iraq) as Abram. As he got older, God told him that he would become the father of a client-nation to God. His offspring would live in the Promised Land of Canaan (Genesis 12:7). In response to God, Abram traveled through the land as far as the site of the great tree of Moreh at Shechem. At that time, the Canaanites were in the land. The Lord appeared to Abram and said, "To your offspring I will give this land" (Genesis 12:7).

Abram's response? He built an altar and worshipped (presumably with a sacrifice) to the Lord (v. 8).

He kept traveling. God promised: "All the land that you see I will give to you and your offspring forever. I will make your offspring like the dust of the earth, so that if anyone could count the dust, then your offspring could be counted" (Genesis 13:16).

Abram's response? He built an altar to the Lord there (v. 18).

Do you get the idea? God blessed Abraham, and his response was to worship and give.

When he left for Canaan, God told Abraham not to bring his relatives. His nephew Lot wanted to go with him. Abram took him along and several challenges resulted from that decision: disputes between their shepherds led to Abram ending up with the lesser piece of land; Lot's household and family were captured by Kedorlaomer, the Elamite king; Lot's wife turned into a pillar of salt after not obeying the angel who told them not to look back on Sodom. This ultimately led to Lot getting drunk and impregnating his two daughters, whose children became the Ammonites and Midianites, who troubled Israel for centuries. The point here is wrong decisions can be carried down for generations.

Indeed, Moab—generally identified with Jordan—frequently clashed with Israel in the years to come. They worshipped Chemosh. Ammon worshipped Molech and practiced child sacrifices. Both Ammon and Moab frequently fought with Israel over the centuries.

Here, we learn of a great decision:

> When Abram heard that his nephew Lot had been captured, he mobilized the 318 trained men who had been born into his household. Then he pursued Kedorlaomer's army until he caught up with them at Dan. There he divided his men and attacked during the night. Kedorlaomer's army fled, but Abram chased them as far as Hobah, north of Damascus. Abram recovered all the goods that had been taken, and he brought back his nephew Lot with his possessions and all the women and other captives (Genesis 14:14–16 NLT).

Points To consider:

What did God give to Abram?

What was Abram's response?

What did God then give to Abram?

What then was Abram's response?

What was the theme illustrated in this give and take?

Abraham disobeyed God but was blessed anyway. Still, the disobedience had consequences which are still playing out in the Middle East and throughout the world today.

Abraham and Melchizedek (Part 2)

After Abram returned from defeating Kedorlaomer and the kings allied with him, the King of Sodom came out to meet him in the Valley of Shaveh (that is, the King's Valley).

Then Melchizedek King of Salem brought out bread and wine. He was priest of God Most High, and he blessed Abram, saying, "Blessed be Abram by God Most High, Creator of heaven and earth. And praise be to God Most High, who delivered your enemies into your hand.

Then Abram gave him a tenth of everything.

The king of Sodom said to Abram, "Give me the people and keep the goods for yourself."

But Abram said to the king of Sodom, "With raised hand I have sworn an oath to the Lord, God Most High, Creator of heaven and earth, that I will accept nothing belonging to you, not even a thread or the strap of a sandal, so that you will never be able to say, 'I made Abram rich.' I will accept nothing but what my men have eaten and the share that belongs to the men who went with me—to Aner, Eshkol and Mamre. Let them have their share (Genesis 14:17–24).

Abram wouldn't accept anything from the King of Sodom.

In the passage, it appears God strongly indicated Abraham should avoid anything related to Sodom (perhaps this message should have been communicated to Lot's wife more forcefully). Interacting with Sodom is a road to destruction. During this time, Abram was totally focused on God. He could tell Melchizedek was from God and the King of Sodom was not. Sodom was already known as a corrupt city filled with wickedness. Allowing Sodom to have people to exploit in an evil city was not in line with Abraham's character. As to Melchizedek, Abraham could discern the prophetic importance of this encounter with God's emissary, having spoken with God directly before. He could tell Melchizedek was divine or at least on God's team.

Points To Consider:

Abram embraced Melchizedek but would take nothing from Sodom. Why is that?

Who, like Sodom, wants the people and not the things of life?

How did Abram discern Melchizedek from Sodom?

Abraham and Melchizedek (Part 3)

Melchizedek is described as "resembling the Son of God" (Hebrews 7:3 ESV). Indeed, later in the same chapter, Jesus is described as: "a priest forever, after the order of Melchizedek" (v. 17). Melchizedek seems to be like a pre-incarnate version of Christ.

Why was Melchizedek necessary? It goes back to the reality that God is perfect and can have nothing to do with the imperfect. After the Fall of Adam and Eve, the God-human relationship was broken. God's ability to interact with fallen, imperfect humankind was limited, since God can have nothing to do with imperfection. His justice is as much a part of His essence as His omniscience, omnipresence, and omnipotence. God cannot compromise.

Praise God for that! Would you really want a God who is not perfect, is slack in His actions, or practices favoritism? God can no more compromise His essence by compromising His justice than He could compromise His love.

An intermediary was needed: in this case, Melchizedek.

When Christ came, He became the perfect lamb, and His sacrifice blessed all of us for all time. Among other things, that bridge to a relationship between God and humankind was established forever.

Back in Abram's time, roughly 2,000 years before the incarnate Christ, Melchizedek, a Christ-type, was the bridge God used to interact with Abram and to accept his sacrifice. Melchizedek, used by God, blessed Abram. He reminded Abram that from God's blessings, Abram was victorious over a larger, more experienced force. God gave Abram the strength, strategy, and favor to defeat a more experienced and equipped foe. Abram realized it was God's victory for him and not his efforts that succeeded. Abraham's response? Abraham gave Melchizedek a tenth of everything he had won, his increase. This set the pattern for tithing that was eventually legislated into Levitical law some 430 years later.

Why Give a Tenth?

Before Abraham, there is no reason to believe that giving a tenth to God was part of His plan or to be a common part of God's relationship to humankind. Then, Melchizedek blessed Abram, and Abram gave him a tenth of everything. The tenth was given in response to God's blessings. It was an act of worship.

Think of the overwhelming awe of that moment. The God of the universe had orchestrated a victory for this man. God had given the Promised Land to Abram and his family for posterity. He had just rescued his kinsmen and his friends and servants. His recognition of God in His life was complete in reverence, gratitude, worship, and thanksgiving.

What could he do except give God a tenth of what God had provided? Stay with me here: A man authorized by God (Melchizedek) to bless a man on God's behalf (Abram) blesses that man whom God chose to father His people, through whom all people will be blessed. This is an extremely significant moment, as it eventually leads to the Jewish nation and to Jesus, our Savior, bridging a right relationship between God and humankind.

Ponder this fact and that moment.

Abram did not grow up worshipping the Lord. His father's household were idol worshippers and did not know the true God. God has chosen Abram, soon to be Abraham, to be the father of His people chosen to reveal the true God to the rest of humanity.

Abraham's action, giving a tenth of everything from his victory, was generated from Melchizedek. Melchizedek acted like Jesus in this encounter, acting as the go-between for God and humankind. God could not have a direct encounter with a sinful man at that period. Perfection could not associate with the imperfect, or God would have to compromise His perfection—an impossible task for Him.

Here, a "Christ-like incarnation," Melchizedek, acted as an intermediary between God and humankind. Later, through animal sacrifices, the separation between God and humankind could be indirectly broached by the blood "covering" the sins, allowing an instance-by-instance relationship.

It wasn't until Christ's death and resurrection that our sins were forgiven because of the blood of the Lamb, Jesus, and never remembered again by God. That last sentence is worth a praise to the Lord. Hallelujah!

That is why Melchizedek was necessary. God could not directly deal with Abram and Melchizedek who, like Jesus two thousand years later, acted as the intermediary for this very important event.

Counterpoint

Some argue that Abraham's gift of 10% of his increase is not a reason to give 10% today. They say the spoils of war were a one-time thing and that lots of people back then gave 10% to their kings to show respect and loyalty. They discount somewhat Abraham's fervor for the Lord, but by accepting 10%, God is asking no more than what a worldly king would have expected. Abraham gave 10% out of gratitude and worship, and God accepted it as such.

If worldly kings were accepting 10%, wouldn't God have the right to require more? Of course He could, but He was not after tribute; He was after Abraham's heart. The giving of the 10% tribute was not as important as the reverence and worship Abraham showed. Considering Abraham's action, 10% was enough.

Points To Consider:

Why was Melchizedek necessary in this story?

With Abraham's success at Kedorlaomer and Melchizedek's representation for God, Abraham's gift of a tenth pleases God. Why was God pleased?

Why was a gift of 10% enough to satisfy God?

In this story, how does Abraham's 10% communicate his love for God?

Abraham and Isaac

Isaac plays two main parts heading into the Jewish age. First, he was the child of the promise. Abraham's firstborn was Ishmael, a child from Hagar. Abraham was getting old. Sarai began to doubt she could deliver a child. She had a handmaid named Hagar and basically said to Abraham, "Let's help God out by taking matters into our own hands and you have a son with Hagar." Abraham obliged, Ishmael was born of Hagar, and God didn't talk to Abraham for 13 years. Abraham's life and his family were in constant squabbles without peace. Sarah told Abraham to kick Hagar and her child out. He did. Hagar and Ishmael ended up parched and starving in the desert until refreshed by an angel, who told Hagar of the child's destiny. Nearly all Middle Eastern families who are not Jews can trace their lineage through Ishmael up to Abraham.

Isaac was finally born when Abraham (formerly "Abram") was one hundred years old and Sarah (formerly "Sarai") was 90 years old. That was a miracle in itself.

Later, God calls upon Abraham and tells him to sacrifice Isaac to Him. Abraham dearly loved Isaac, but the next morning (note his prompt compliance with God's command, showing his reliance on the Lord by faith), they head towards the mountains near Salem (later to be "Jerusalem"). With them are two servants.

Abraham has a lot to digest. He loves the boy, but God has said to sacrifice him. He knows that Isaac is the child of the promise, the line of the future, leading to the Jewish people. Hebrews 7 tells us that Abraham is wondering, perhaps if the boy is killed, God will resurrect him? Does this idea sound familiar?

Nearing the mountain, Abraham tells the servants to keep watch as the two of them proceed to the mountains for the sacrifice. Along the way, Isaac observes to his father that they have everything needed for a sacrifice but the sacrifice itself. Abraham responds that the Lord will provide.

They get to the place of the sacrifice in the mountains. Preparations are completed. Isaac is placed on the altar; the knife is drawn and ready. God then tells Abraham to stop. God and Abraham recognize that Abraham loves God more than anything, even to the death of the promised son. A stray ram is then sacrificed in Isaac's place.

Several things to note here: For Abraham so loved the Lord that he was ready to give his promised child to remain in proper relationship with the Lord God almighty. Can you think of a parallel here, say John 3:16?

Second, this is a test of Abraham, who is to be the father of many nations. God wanted someone committed to Him, and Abraham passed with flying colors. Abraham, by faith, gave. Tithing (prior to the Law and then again, after) follows that same pattern.

Finally, the whole saga of Ishmael, who is Abraham's firstborn by the Law, and Isaac, the firstborn of the promise, foretells the greater position of the child of grace compared to the child of the Law. Grace is greater, as we will see with the birth of the Christ, our Lord Jesus. As such, Isaac is greater than Ishmael, as the promised child will come from Him.

With the passing of this test, the time of the Israelites is near.

Points To Consider:

What did Abraham need to sacrifice Isaac besides the equipment they carried?

Who else was to be later sacrificed in Jerusalem?

Why did this test even occur?

How did the many gifts that Abraham had received during his life prepare him for the potential sacrifice?

How is Abraham's relationship with God evidenced in this scene?

What is the importance of faith in this event?

Abraham's faith had matured as he matured. He saw many incredible gifts from God, and those gifts prepared him to continue being faithful.

Jacob (Part 1)

God chose Abraham to be the father of many nations. He chose the lineage of Isaac over Ishmael, as Isaac was the son promised to Sarah and Abraham. Ishmael, the son of Abraham and Hagar, was Abraham's first child, the child of Abraham's self-effort.

Isaac fathered twins, Esau and Jacob. Jacob, the younger twin and the child chosen of God to be the father of His chosen people, the Israelites, started out as an unlikely choice to lead Abraham's people—and eventually, the world—into a personal relationship with God the Father almighty.

Jacob meant "supplanter," trickster," "circumventer," or even "cheater." In his youth, he lived up to those descriptions. He came from a family who were aptly described with these names. He basically stole his brother's birthright in exchange for a bowl of soup (Esau was hungry, and Jacob took advantage of him, an act likely unenforceable as egregious if they went to court today). His mother helped him trick his father into bestowing his brother Esau's blessing on Jacob by dressing him in his brother's clothes and covering him with goat hair to simulate his brother's hairy skin. Esau's (understandable) response sent Jacob fleeing to his Uncle Laban's house. As he was running away to escape his brother's wrath, Jacob had time to think about his life.

Was the life of a cheat really the life he wanted to live? Life as a cheat was taking its toll on him; he had to run, and he had to stay ahead of anyone chasing after him. This was not the life of peace.

How does this apply to tithing? As Jacob was escaping his brother's anger, he made a vow, "If God will be with me and will watch over me on this journey I am taking and will give me food to eat and clothes to wear so that I return safely to my father's household, then the LORD will be my God and this stone that I have set up as a pillar will be God's house, and of all that you give me I will give you a tenth" (Genesis 28:20–22).

At first blush, this sounds like a guy bartering with God: If you give me this and that, I will give you 5%—no, 10%!—of my money. Believe me, I have tried that in my own life, and it doesn't work. God doesn't need your money.

What we have here is a man on the run, scared and sick of the way he has led his life. He is now turning to God, the God he has never really experienced. Along the journey to his new life, he has time to reflect on the kind of life he has been living. He knows through the tales of his grandfather Abraham and father Isaac that following God is the right way to live. He wants to change his life, and he is seeking God. He wants his new life to be a success. He doesn't quite know the right way to ask but he is begging God from the depth of his heart: do this Lord and I am yours, and I will give you a tenth, just like my grandad Abraham told me he did when you gave him victory near Salem.

Jacob is seeking a relationship with God, and God always answers such a request even if it is not necessarily "properly worded." This is Jacob's first shot at a prayer seeking God. God looks to the heart and sees Jacob wants a relationship with Him. That is God's ultimate desire for all of us, generated by love. And now, we have another instance where worship includes a pattern of giving 10%, an amount not yet codified in Levitical law but certainly acceptable to God, not as a bargain but as a heartfelt attempt of a struggling man to get right with God.

Points To Consider:

How is Jacob's offer not legalism or bargaining with God?

Is God moved by this heartfelt desire for a relationship with Him?

Does God show that grace today for those wanting a relationship with Him?

Giving a 10th is referenced. Do you think that figure might have come from what Jacob had heard from Abraham?

How does God bless Jacob with this heartfelt request?

Jacob (Part 2)

Jacob's line is chosen to lead the world to God the Father. Before Jacob can become Israel, there will be about 20 years of maturing. When he lived in his parents' house, Jacob was the cheater, the one taking advantage of others. His mother's guidance helped refine those skills. Now, he finds himself in the world of Laban, his mother's brother and Jacob's uncle, with his sons and daughters (including Leah and Rachel) and their handmaidens, all of whom take advantage of him. His Uncle Laban was also a cheat and cheated Jacob into marrying his less attractive older daughter, Leah, when the two had bargained for the more attractive Rachel. Laban and his sons cheated Jacob several times in their dealings with livestock.

Jacob is cheated by his family for the entire 20 years he lives away, until the time is right for Jacob to return home and reconcile with his brother. Perhaps it was because he wanted to go home to Canaan, the land of his youth, that made him want to make things right, particularly with his brother Esau. Perhaps having spent 20 years surrounded by connivers and cheats of varying degrees, he just wanted to lead a more righteous life or to learn of the God of his father and grandfather. His wives Leah and Rachel dished up their own flavor of trouble in their constant squabbles and bargaining. Whatever the reasons, Jacob decides to go home.

Leaving involved a confrontation with his Uncle Laban that could have ended badly. Rachel, the wife he loved, had stolen from her father the family idols, and Jacob promised to have the thief killed. It is only Rachel's trickery that keeps her alive.

On the way to Canaan, Jacob encounters the pre-incarnate Christ, just like Abraham did with Melchizedek two generations before. Only now, Jacob wrestles the angel all night long. As the angel gets ready to leave, Jacob calls on Him to bless Him. He does so by changing his name to Israel and striking his hip bone out of the socket, leaving him with a permanent limp. So began the chosen people of God. As he gets older and sees the error of always trying to pull a fast one, Jacob, now known as Israel, seeks a better relationship with God, exactly what God desired with the first of His chosen people.

Jacob was bold in asking for a blessing. You should come to God in the same way.

Jacob (Part 3)

Word soon comes to Jacob, the recently renamed Israel, that his brother Esau is traveling towards the group. Israel strategically separates his family into two groups, just in case Esau is coming for vengeance so that perhaps one group could escape an attack. He further sends lead parties with gifts ahead of the main party, seeking to placate his brother. Finally, they meet face-to-face. Esau has the superior force and is quite capable of wiping his younger brother out. What does he choose?

> But Esau ran to meet Jacob and embraced him; he threw his arms around his neck and kissed him. And they wept. Then Esau looked up and saw the women and children. "Who are these with you?" he asked. Jacob answered, "They are the children God has graciously given your servant" (Genesis 33:4-5).

One of those children was Joseph, who witnessed this interchange from the front row. Decades later, Joseph had a similar encounter with his brothers after he became second-in-command of Egypt, a development in his life that began with his brothers selling him to traders out of jealousy of him. Joseph responded with weeping and forgiveness, just like Esau.

Israel's sons proved to be a source of agitation and sorrow late into his life. Reuben slept with one of his wives. Simeon and Levi massacred the Hamorites, defending their sister Dinah's honor, making it necessary for the family to flee their new homestead. All of his sons, except Benjamin, conspired first to kill Joseph, then to sell him into slavery, and then lie about it for at least 13 years.

It was only late in life that Jacob, now Israel, saw the unfolding of God's plan and his position in God's handiwork. His offspring, Jesus, was to lead the world to God.

Points To Consider:

How large of a transition was necessary for Jacob/Israel to go from a cheater to a reconciler?

What about for Esau? How did he evolve?

How do you think that Israel's continuing towards Esau was necessary for God to use him and his people?

"He cuts off every branch in me that bears no fruit, while every branch that does bear fruit he prunes so that it will be even more fruitful" (John 15:2). How might this be an example of God using testing to sharpen Israel?

What was Israel's response in this looming encounter? (See Genesis 32:9–12)

How did he have the strength to meet his brother, knowing things could have turned out a lot differently and decidedly worse?

In an act of faith and repentance, Jacob, the cheater and supplanter, gave gifts to the one he cheated, furthering his transformation into God's chosen, Israel.

From Abraham to Moses

Abraham begat Isaac and many other children. Isaac begat Jacob and Esau, but our focus is on Jacob, who later became Israel. Israel had 12 sons and at least one daughter (Dinah). Judah became the line to David and Jesus, but for this passage, let's take a moment to examine Levi.

Jacob, now Israel, settled things with his brother Esau and proceeded to Canaan, the Promised Land. He bought a parcel of land near Shechem for one hundred pieces of silver and began the process of moving in, including an altar to God, el elohe ("the God who provides").

Dinah went out to meet the women of the land and was promptly raped by Shechem, the son of Hamor, the leading citizen of the area. Shechem insisted his father strike a deal to have Dinah as his bride.

He pointed out the benefits of joining economically with Jacob and the Israelites.

When word of the rape got to Israel, he was silent until his sons returned from the field. When they heard of the incident, they were all outraged. Still, when Shechem's father proposed marriage, they listened. They made it clear that they could not intermarry with any group that was not circumcised. The Hamorites discussed it and agreed to be circumcised if that meant expanding their economy.

While they were nursing themselves post-circumcision, Simeon and Levi, two of Jacob's sons, killed every male in the town and brought their sister back. When Jacob heard this, he was furious. They took all the women and children of Shechem, along with all their goods and livestock, and, at God's direction, moved to Bethel.

But Jacob did not forgive the acts of Simeon and Levi, and on his death bed, he cursed them.

> "Simeon and Levi are brothers—their swords are weapons of violence. Let me not enter their council, let me not join their assembly, for they have killed men in their anger and hamstrung oxen as they pleased. Cursed be their anger, so fierce, and their fury, so cruel! I will scatter them in Jacob and disperse them in Israel" (Genesis 49:5–7).

Ouch. That's not the kind of farewell one hopes for from Dad.

Fast forward about four hundred years later, Moses has just received the two stone tablets containing the Ten Commandments when he hears partying in the camp. He sees the golden calf they are worshipping, and he is filled with anger.

He first interacts with God hoping to keep him from destroying everyone. Then he turns his attention to the people.

> When Moses approached the camp and saw the calf and the dancing, his anger burned and he threw the tablets out of his hands, breaking them to pieces at the foot of the mountain. And he took the calf the people had made and burned

it in the fire; then he grounded it to powder, scattered it on the water and made the Israelites drink it (Exodus 32:19–20).

Moses, angry and disgusted, provides the climax to this vile debauchery.

Moses saw that the people were running wild and that Aaron had let them get out of control and so become a laughing-stock to their enemies. So he stood at the entrance to the camp and said, "Whoever is for the Lord, come to me." And all the Levites rallied to him.

Then he said to them, "This is what the Lord, the God of Israel, says: 'Each man strap a sword to his side. Go back and forth through the camp from one end to the other, each killing his brother and friend and neighbor.'" The Levites did as Moses commanded, and that day about three thousand of the people died. Then Moses said, "You have been set apart to the Lord today, for you were against your own sons and brothers, and he has blessed you this day" (Genesis 33:25–29).

The Levites, scorned by Jacob, later became the keepers of the Law. This happened when they followed Moses, quenching God's anger, even to the death of their kinsmen.

Interestingly enough, the day the Ten Commandments were delivered, three thousand people died. When Pentecost occurred, beginning the church age, three thousand people were saved (Acts 2:41). Grace exceeds the Law. The Savior is greater than the Law.

Points To Consider:

Were the Levites hotheads in wiping out the Hamorites? What did it get them from their heavenly father?

Were the Levites hotheads when they killed three thousand of their fellow tribesmen? What did it get them from their heavenly father?

What does "grace exceeds the Law" mean to you?

Tithing Under the Law

What is Levitical Law?

The Levitical Law, also known as the Mosaic Law, was given to Moses. He was a Levite, known as a son of Levi; one of the 12 tribes of Israel. God gave the Mosaic Law to Moses on Mount Sinai. The Levites were chosen as the tribe responsible for religious duties for the nation, based on their zeal in following God and Moses in wiping out the golden calf episode.[1]

God explained the purpose of the Law as a covenant, a binding agreement between God and the Israelites: "Now if you obey me fully and keep my covenant, then out of all nations you will be my treasured possession. Although the whole earth is mine, you will be for me a kingdom of priests and a holy nation" (Exodus 19:5–6).

The difficulty was that the Israelites were to obey all 613 laws, not just the Ten Commandments (which would be hard enough!) to receive the benefits of the Law.

"The people all responded together, 'We will do everything the LORD has said'" (Exodus 19:8). So, Moses brought their answer back

---

1. "Levitical Law," "Mosaic Law," and "Old Testament Law" all refer to the Ten Commandments and the 603 other laws (think of that—613 Laws to be followed explicitly in daily living) found in the Book of Leviticus. We will use all terms interchangeably or simply refer to it as "the Law."

to the Lord. This prideful response (including the Law) lasted 1,500 years with millions dying in their arrogance and self-effort.

The Purpose of Levitical Law?

The Mosaic Law was given specifically to the nation of Israel (Exodus 19–20). "These are the decrees, regulations, and instructions that the Lord gave through Moses on Mount Sinai as evidence of the relationship between himself and the Israelites" (Leviticus 26:46 NLT). The "decrees" (the Ten Commandments), "regulations" (the ordinances), and "instructions" (for the priests, the offerings and for worship) constitute the 613 laws required to be followed by the Mosaic Law.

Much was required from God's chosen people in keeping the Mosaic Law. They had been chosen to spread the knowledge of God throughout the Earth. The people of Israel were "chosen to be God's adopted children. God revealed his glory to them. He made covenants with them and gave them His law. He gave them the privilege of worshiping him and receiving his wonderful promises" (Romans 9:4 NLT). Through the following of the Law, they were to be blessed, a city on a hill for other people to recognize their blessed life because they were God's adopted children. This adoption required them to "be holy because I, the LORD your God, am holy" (Leviticus 19:2 NLT). The Law set apart the nation of Israel as distinct from all the other nations, signifying they were God's chosen people. As God had chosen them to be His people, they needed to act like His chosen people, unique and uniquely blessed. The actions required by the Mosaic Law reflected back on the people of Israel as well. Following God's instructions brought them closer to God, revealing His essence to them: "Now if you will obey me and keep my covenant, you will be my own special treasure from among all the peoples on earth; for all the earth belongs to me" (Exodus 19:5 NLT).

The Law was "holy, and the commandment [was] holy, righteous and good" (Romans 7:12). It provided a way of worship for the community of faith through the observance of yearly feasts (Leviticus 23), the most significant and holiest being Yom Kippur, or the Day of Atonement. On this day, blood from sacrificed animals covered their sins, allowing God to interact with people. There were other occasions on which sacrifices were made, but Yom Kippur remained the most significant for the entirety of the nation of Israel.

Perhaps crucial to their longevity despite thousands of years of persecution, the Law provided God's direction for the physical and spiritual health of the nation. In fact, the sanitary laws may have actually provided protection against the European bubonic plague during the Dark Ages, which led to persecution by their neighbors. And, perhaps most importantly, the sacrifices and offerings required by the Law provided forgiveness for the people who had faith in the Lord in the nation of Israel (Leviticus 1–7). However, it still fell short.

Tithing and Giving Under the Law

We have seen that giving goes back before the Law, all the way back to Cain and Abel. Before the Law, Abraham gave a tenth of his spoils of battle to Melchizedek, who served as God's intermediary to receive Abraham's giving. But it wasn't until 1450 BC that tithing was codified into Levitical law. *Giving* became optional, but *tithing* was required. Giving and tithing are two different things. Giving functions in both the Old and New Testaments. Tithing as practiced in Old Testament times was sanctioned by God for the client state of Israel. God commanded Israel to tithe (Leviticus 27:30–34) as a form of national taxation. Tithes were placed on Jewish believers and non-believers. The tithe, or "tenth," was calculated on what you owned or received from your labors.

There were several types of tithes:

1. A tax for maintaining the Levites (Numbers 18:21–24)

2. A tax for national feasts and sacrifices (Deuteronomy 14:22–27)

3. A tax every third year for the benefit of the nation's poor and destitute (Deuteronomy 14:28–29)

Old Testament tithing was not the same as giving, and it varied from the tenth given before Israel became a client state to God. Tithing in the nation-state of Israel was not done as free will. Tithing combined both spiritual and civil functions. As a theocracy—a nation ruled by God—every person, believer and non-believer, was required to support the nation through tithing.

Giving went beyond the requirement to pay taxes for the maintenance of the nation. A gift requires free will, centered on the willingness to honor what God has provided. "One person gives freely, yet gains even more; another withholds unduly, but comes to poverty. A generous person will prosper; whoever refreshes others will be refreshed" (Proverbs 11:24–25).

Only the believer was properly motivated to give above tithe.

As mentioned, with the introduction of the Law, tithing was formalized and became mandatory. Do this and be blessed. Don't do this and be separated from God and His blessings. This illustrates the beauty and exasperation of the Law. Under the Law, people offered blood sacrifices to atone for their sins. This covered the sins but did not last beyond the last sacrifice. Even now, Jews celebrate the Day of Atonement, the day of sacrifice for all the last year's sins. Still, if you go out into the parking lot and someone cuts you off, you carry that sin of cussing them out into the next year. That is a long time to live under the guilt of sin.

Entering the Promised Land

After 430 years of slavery, God told the Israelites to ask the Egyptians for their jewels, gold, and fine raiment to be given to their children on the way out of Egypt. The parents may have had a slave mentality coming out of the centuries of enslavement, but the children were to be blessed with a new self-image: one of the blessings of being God's children. They left Egypt and arrived at the Red Sea. There, they faced Pharoah and his six hundred chariots, which seemingly promised death. People were upset and squawking fearful complaints at Moses. Then, God said to Moses "Raise your staff and stretch out your hand over the sea to divide the water so that the Israelites can go through the sea on dry ground" (Exodus 14:16).

And Moses raised his staff, stretched out his hand, and the sea parted in front of them. The Israelites passed through the corridor of water walls safely. The Egyptians didn't fare as well; six hundred charioteers and their support staff and horses died. And so began the nation of Israel. A family of roughly 69 people went into Egypt, and a ragtag group of around two million came out 430 years later. Now, would they fulfill the promise God gave them to take the Promised Land?

God wanted to show mankind the blessings He was ready to bestow. He chose the Jews as the people to bless so that other peoples would want to be like them. After years of slavery in Egypt, the children of Abraham were "chosen" by God as His special people to show the rest of the world how great a relationship with Him could be. As we have discussed, in order to show the world the benefits of living unto the Lord, God instituted the Ten Commandments and the Law around 1500 B.C. This is how tithing operated under that system in the Promised Land.

The Law, in the form of the Ten Commandments, was given to Moses around 1450 BC.

God had summoned Moses and told him that the Israelites would be God's treasured possession if they followed His rules. The people all responded together, "'We will do everything the Lord has said.' So, Moses brought their answer back to the Lord" (Exodus 19:8).

God called Moses up Mount Sinai, and Moses received the Law. Then, Moses came down the mountain with the tablets, only to hear riotous partying and sin. His delivery of the tablets ended in anger, with Moses throwing the original tablets down and the Levites joining Moses in killing three thousand people to quell God's wrath (Exodus 32). That confidence in their self-effort brought about the golden calf. They took their dependence off God, relied on self-effort, and brought about disaster.

Jericho

The first city to be taken was Jericho. Jericho was a bulwark of a high-walled city with homes and fortifications inside the walls, protecting the residents and the other cities along the Israelites path.

God told the Israelites to walk around the city for seven days, silently, one time per day for the first six days. On the seventh day, they walked around the city seven times, blew their trumpets, and shouted on the final lap.

What happened? "Joshua fit the battle of Jericho, and the walls came tumbling down!"[2]

Now, God also told them to gather up the spoils and give them all to God. Why? Because this was to be the tithe of firstfruits to God for his blessing them with the victory and the victories to come, where they could keep the spoils. However, a man named Achan saw

---

2. https://www.oxfordlearnersdictionaries.com/us/definition/english/joshua-fit-the-battle-of-jericho

some precious metal and a beautiful coat and took them, in direct disobedience to God.

When the Israelites went to take the next city, fully confident in their military prowess and God's blessing, they got whipped by a much inferior force. They came back crying and complaining. God told them to shut up and to come out as one tribe, one family, one man, to determine the culprit who caused the loss. Achan was caught. Achan confessed. The people ran to his tent to confirm what he said.

> Then Joshua, together with all Israel, took Achan son of Zerah, the silver, the robe, the gold bar, his sons and daughters, his cattle, donkeys and sheep, his tent and all that he had, to the Valley of Achor. Joshua said, "Why have you brought this trouble on us? The Lord will bring trouble on you today."
>
> Then all Israel stoned him, and after they had stoned the rest, they burned them. Over Achan they heaped up a large pile of rocks, which remains to this day. Then the Lord turned from his fierce anger. Therefore that place has been called the Valley of Achor ever since (Joshua 7:24-26).

God takes tithing seriously. Jericho was to be the tithe of first-fruits for the conquering of the rest of the cities. By not tithing, the lesson became a curse with dire consequences for the man who did not follow God's plan.

The people learned an important lesson about tithing that day.

After conquering Jericho and the other cities of the Promised Land, the land was divided amongst the 12 tribes of Israel. "In those days ... everyone did what was right in his own eyes" (Judges 21:25 NKJV). Eventually, a king was demanded, and despite warning His people that this was a colossally bad idea, God allowed them their king and all of the problems that came with it.

Phineas and Hophni

Eli was the judge of Israel before Samuel, a kind of quasi-leader but full-time priest. Israel had no king from about 1450 BC until Saul ascended the throne. King Saul ruled Israel from 1047 BC to 1007 BC. For the first 39 or so years of that reign, Samuel was the judge of Israel. When Saul and his sons were killed in battle with the Philistines, David became king.

Eli had two sons, Phineas and Hophni. They were the logical people to succeed him as judge, but God had other plans. They didn't succeed their father in part because they never recognized the seriousness and importance of the office. Indeed, they treated their positions crassly, not as the potential future spiritual leaders of Israel. They didn't honor their awesome lineage and blessing.

Worse, Eli didn't discipline them in a manner appropriate for Israel's future judges and high priests. Eli's failure to instill righteousness in his children led to the destruction of the family line. "Now Eli, who was very old, heard about everything his sons were doing to all Israel and how they slept with the women who served at the entrance to the tent of meeting"(1 Samuel 2:22).

Sleeping with women who work for you and abusing a position of power would lead to job termination and maybe prison in today's America. Eli did nothing. And it got worse.

> Eli's sons were scoundrels; they had no regard for the Lord. Now it was the practice of the priests that, whenever any of the people offered a sacrifice, the priest's servant would come with a three-pronged fork in his hand while the meat was being boiled and would plunge the fork into the pan or kettle or caldron or pot. Whatever the fork brought up the priest would take for himself. This is how they treated all the Israelites who came to Shiloh. But even before the fat was burned, the priest's servant would come and say to the person who was sacrificing, "Give the priest some meat to roast; he won't accept boiled meat from you, but only raw."

If the person said to him, "Let the fat be burned first, and then take whatever you want," the servant would answer, "No, hand it over now; if you don't, I'll take it by force." This sin of the young men was very great in the Lord's sight, for they were treating the Lord's offering with contempt (1 Samuel 2:12–17).

More importantly, they were disrespecting God and the tithe. They took God's portion of the tithe offered by others and applied it to themselves with full knowledge that was wrong. Perhaps more arrogantly, they knew after the fat portion was cooked, they could share in the tithe as Eli's sons. By taking the tithe earlier, before it was fully cooked, they were taking more than their share - robbing God.

How did God respond? Eli's sons died the same day in a battle. When Eli heard of it, he fell back in his chair and broke his neck and also died. God had told Eli this would happen; He also said that none of Eli's male heirs would ever live to an old age. And none of them did.

Point To Consider

It is still not a good policy to rob God.

Elijah, a Woman, and a Cake

One of the worst royal couples in history may be Ahab and Jezebel. Think about it—many families have women named Sarah or Mary or Elizabeth. Jezebel? Not so much. The reason is this couple was so consumed with worshipping false gods that God had to interject and eventually deal with them. Ahab was supernaturally killed by an arrow shot into the air that God directed into an opening in his armor, early in a battle. By the day's end, he was dead.

Jezebel, all dolled up, was thrown out of a window and before they could clean the mess up, the dogs had eaten her. This act fulfilled a prophecy.

But let's go back. There had been Elijah, God's messenger, who sought to convince Ahab of the error of his ways.

Elijah was a major force for God in the Old Testament, despite suffering from depression and at least once from conceit, which God had to refine him through to use him for His will.

Elijah announced to Ahab and all of Israel that it will not rain again until he, Elijah, announces the rain's return.

Then, he runs. He runs to a ravine where God says He will supernaturally feed him by ravens bringing him food and he drinks from the brook. The brook eventually dries up, and God tells him to go to Zarephath.

Some time later the brook dried up because there had been no rain in the land. Then the word of the Lord came to him: "Go at once to Zarephath in the region of Sidon and stay there. I have directed a widow there to supply you with food." So he went to Zarephath. When he came to the town gate, a widow was there gathering sticks. He called to her and asked, "Would you bring me a little water in a jar so I may have a drink?" As she was going to get it, he called, "And bring me, please, a piece of bread."

"As surely as the Lord your God lives," she replied, "I don't have any bread—only a handful of flour in a jar and a little olive oil in a jug. I am gathering a few sticks to take home and make a meal for myself and my son, that we may eat it—and die."

Elijah said to her, "Don't be afraid. Go home and do as you have said. But first make a small loaf of bread for me from what you have and bring it to me, and then make something for yourself and your son. For this is what the Lord, the God of Israel, says: 'The jar of flour will not be used up and the jug of oil will not run dry until the day the Lord sends rain on the land.'"

She went away and did as Elijah had told her. So there was food every day for Elijah and for the woman and her family. For the jar of flour was not used up and the jug of oil did not run dry, in keeping with the word of the Lord spoken by Elijah (1 Kings 17:7–16).

God sent Elijah to take care of her, not for Elijah's care. God arranged the scene so that His representative, Elijah (who was hungry), asks her for bread. She complies, putting Elijah before her and her child. God then blesses her far beyond anything she could have expected or imagined.

God wants you to tithe to take care of you, not just financially but your business, your health, and your family. She gave not knowing the results, and God blessed her mightily for it. Get all your priorities in order, and by tithing, you are in the same position of this woman.

Both the woman and Elijah were blessed by this encounter. The woman saw the glory of God work in her life while being physically saved. That salvation was throughout the drought, showing her daily God's love and concern for her.

Elijah was comforted by seeing God's work in her life. He was the instrument God used to bring blessings, and this interaction strengthened his reliance on God after his physical and mental fatigue. This interlude prepared him for what he had to do. Besides the sustaining miracle God gave them both during the drought, something else happened; her son got sick and was on the edge of dying. Elijah saved him, strengthened by the faith that this experience had provided.

Later, Elijah outran Ahab's chariot guided by swift horse, brought the rain back, killed four hundred prophets of Baal, and then went on the run again. 1 Kings 19 captures these events. It's a great story but gets a little difficult for Elijah again.

In this story though, we saw a woman whose faith led to giving what she had, and that saved her life and eventually her child's life. Her faith in action (giving) blessed her exceedingly and abundantly (Ephesians 3:20).

The Return From Captivity

The Babylonian captivity lasted 70 years, just as God said it would. As they returned, God directed them to restore the Temple, which was completed in 516 B.C. This allowed the Jews to carry out their ritual service in the sanctuary.

Around 450 BC, the walls of Jerusalem were also rebuilt under the direction of Nehemiah. Malachi appears to have been a contemporary of the governor Nehemiah. Their books cover many common issues, particularly about spiritual purity.

The Jews returned to Judea enthusiastic for worshipping God and rigorously against pagan idol worship. But as time passed, they let their guard down. They slacked off, compromised, and eventually became more accepting to idol worship in their midst, contrary to God's intents and purposes for bringing them back. In the process, they also began to lose sight of God's purposes for them.

According to the Book of Malachi, people were divorcing and mixed marriages were occurring, which was leading to pagan worship. Tithing was not being practiced.

Contemporaneous to this period of Nehemiah becoming the primary civil government ruler, Malachi was sent to instruct and guide God's people toward a purer life.

Malachi was the primary voice telling them their sins were causing God to strip away their physical prosperity and position of influence in the region. Drought, famine, poverty, and oppression from outsiders were their reward for ignoring God and His laws. Moral decay, spiritual compromise, and arrogance led to pride, indifference, permissiveness, and skepticism. "They sow the wind and reap the whirlwind…" (Hosea 8:7).

Only by a nationwide, heartfelt repentance would the blessings of God be restored again. Malachi pleaded with his countrymen to humble themselves in prayer, seeking restoration of God's blessings.

Malachi the Messenger

The span of time between the giving of the Law and the writing of the book of Malachi was about a thousand years. During that time, the essence of the Law could be summed up in "Do good, get good. Do bad, get bad." Unfortunately for the Jews living under the Law, no one is good. That old sin nature has been a part of the DNA of everyone since Adam and Eve and has made full compliance with the Law impossible because "all have sinned and fall short of the glory of God" (Romans 3:23).

Since no one could comply with the Law, animal sacrifices provided the way to bridging the gap between God and humans. The Old Testament is filled with appropriate sacrifices to cover one's sin so that God and humankind could interact. The problem with this approach is that all animal blood could do is *cover* the sin; it did not wash it away.

Additionally, the Law existed to demonstrate to the Jews that they needed a Savior. The Ten Commandments and 603 Levitical laws to obey would have been exhausting. No wonder people became cynical and disaffected. This attitude of cynicism traces throughout the Old Testament. A good king like David led to a fabulous time of prosperity during Solomon's rule. But after a generation or two, a series of mostly bad kings (though sometimes just mediocre) ushered in defeat, poverty, and alienation from God.

This cycle continued for about 450 years, until finally, starting in about 605 BC, Babylonian captivity forcibly removed many Jews from the Promised Land. This period lasted about 70 years. During that time, Daniel and other prophets strengthened the people.

Yet the return to the land God had given them did not guarantee a return to God. What started with enthusiasm soon turned into self-interest. People got busy with their own lives and failed (again) to honor God in the manner prescribed by the Law. The prophet Haggai chastises the returnees for not rebuilding the Temple as the top priority. Later, the people bemoan the fact that the newly built Temple was not as grand as the first. (Haggai 1–2)

We should not look down on them for their return to old habits. For one thing, if you returned to your home and land after 70 years, you would probably want to set those things in order. Title disputes, unkempt residences, dangerous animals roaming the streets and houses—your first thoughts might be about yourself and family and the mess you need to clean up. After that, you might want to slack off a little bit after a nine hundred-mile journey to get back home.

Following their parents' lead, it would be easy for the next generations to attend to more secular things and not worship the God who left them exiled them for 70 years.

Even with the joy of the return, everyday life could distract their focus from God and toward themselves. Sadly, this focus on themselves led to marrying non-Jews, divorcing Jewish wives for pagan women, corrupt practices at the synagogue, and a general decline in their morality and with it, their very quality of life.

They became faithless, disobedient, and bitter towards God… and then came Malachi.

Malachi's Word to the Returning Jews

Malachi was a prophet of God sent to the "sons of Jacob" (Malachi 3:6 KJV)—the Jews who had resettled in Judea—and to all Israel in general. Toward the close of the book, it becomes clear that God is also speaking beyond the Jews and to all of humankind. He will not endure man's sins forever, and a day of judgment is coming, but God also reveals through Malachi that He will hold back His wrath if people return to Him.

When the Jews began returning from their 70 years of Babylonian captivity, God directed them to begin restoring Jerusalem and build the second temple, often called Zerubbabel's temple. The completion of the new temple by 516 B.C. allowed the Jews to carry out the ritual services of the sanctuary (Malachi 1:10; 3:10).

A Call for Spiritual Purity

When they first returned to Judea from their captivity in Babylon, the Jews rigorously guarded against pagan idol worship in their land. But over time, they gradually gave in to this sin. In the process, they also began to lose sight of God's purposes for them. It was during this period that Malachi was sent to instruct and guide God's people toward a purer life.

Malachi revealed the spiritual and moral shortcomings of the priests and common people alike. Tithing was being neglected (Malachi 3:7–10), divorce had become commonplace, and there were mixed marriages with pagan peoples. These were serious problems (Malachi 2:10–16).

Their sins were the reason that God was once again removing their prosperity, allowing them to face many trials (Malachi 1:6–10, 12–14; 2:1–9). Malachi called for spiritual purity, begging his people to pray and genuinely repent as a nation, for only then would God restore His blessings (Malachi 1:9).

Nehemiah

Nehemiah was the civil leader joining the restoration Malachi was seeking for the people. He didn't start out that way: When we first meet him, he is an official serving in the court of Artaxerxes, the king of Persia (now Iran).

He was the king's wine taster, a job that put him in proximity to the king daily and over time, showed the king that he was a man who could be trusted. This was a great position to be in as a Jew who is to be used by God.

The book of Nehemiah opens with Nehemiah receiving a report that Jerusalem is in distress; the walls are broken, and the gates are burnt. Nehemiah cries out to the Lord, seeking mercy for God's people.

He appears before the king with a sad face, which the king notices and asks why. Nehemiah explains his sadness, and by the end of the conversation, he is given not just permission to go to Jerusalem and restore his country, but the king makes him a provincial governor and provides everything he needs. Building materials are to be requisitioned from local rulers along the way, military protection along the nine hundred-mile journey is provided, and whatever he needs is to be made available to him, based on letters from the king.

He meets opposition when he gets to Jerusalem in the form of Tobiah and Sanballat, but these two are ultimately overcome after some drama and loss of time. And eventually, Jerusalem is restored.

Despite coming home to Jerusalem with the high rank of its provincial governor, Nehemiah chose to identify with his people, who were suffering and had lost their way. He rebuilt the walls of Jerusalem, opposed Jew-on-Jew oppression, and led the officials and nobles to restore property to the people and return tax money to the oppressed. He ordered the nobles to forgive debts.

As the civil administrator, Nehemiah continued to do what was right in the sight of God. He gathered the people and listed them according to genealogy (Nehemiah 7). He had God's word read to them by Ezra the priest (Nehemiah 8). He restored the land to the people. With Ezra, he brought the people back to God.

Nehemiah wasn't content just to see the walls repaired. He wasn't content just to see the people of Israel come home to their own land. Along with Ezra the priest, Nehemiah worked to bring people back to the Lord (Nehemiah 8:9).

And that included tithing (Nehemiah 10:35–37).

Doing as God directed, including tithing, brought peace and prosperity as the Jews rededicated themselves to honoring God.

Points To Consider:

Are we like those returning Jews in our laxity, indifference, and permissiveness?

Would we act any different than the returning Jews when they returned to the Promise Land after 70 years?

Ask yourself: Do I read God's word more than watch financial shows on TV? Do I make a place for regular church attendance? Are my children and grandchildren learning about Jesus and God's grace like you did as a child? What are you doing to spread God's word, especially for your family?

The Message of the Messenger

The Book of Malachi would be the last word of God for over 400 years, until John the Baptist begins proclaiming the arrival of the Messiah. Malachi ("my messenger") may or may not have been the prophet/writer's true name. He was God's messenger to a society that hadn't changed much from the pre-Babylonian captivity. Their initial enthusiasm for God upon their return devolved into selfishness, disobeying God's rules, and failing God in most ways, including worshipping foreign gods. Despite this continued rebellion and spiritual decline, God wanted to give them hope for the coming of a Savior.

This is the world as Malachi comes on the scene. The book of Malachi is written about one hundred years after the Jews return from exile. It is during a time when another foreign power, Persia, is ruling his intended audience: the people of Judah. We know this from Malachi's use of a Persian word for "ruler," which in turn suggests the book was written around 430 BC.

Malachi delivered his message to Judeans familiar with worshipping in the temple, accusing them of turning away from the one, true God and opening themselves up to judgment, rather than God's true desire to bless them, including with a Savior.

In the Christian Bible, Malachi is the last book of the Old Testament and rightly so. It shows us the heart of a people who have been waiting a long time for a deliverer, a Savior, but who have been led astray during the continual wait.

They have the promise of a Messiah but the reality of wandering in the desert and the shame of exile from the Promised Land. They continually demonstrate that humans cannot follow the Law and that a Savior who can is necessary to make things right with God, a Lamb worthy of sacrifice for all.

The book of Malachi sums up what the whole Hebrew Bible has been pointing to—God's people cannot be faithful to the covenant. They've failed again and again. After a long period of separation from God with immorality and corruption, they are spiritually numb and alienated. Fortunately, while God will deal with their sin, he will not abandon them. He promises to redeem a remnant and send a Messiah to fulfill his covenant promises.

"I the LORD do not change. So you, the descendants of Jacob, are not destroyed. Ever since the time of your ancestors you have turned away from my decrees and have not kept them. Return to me, and I will return to you," says the Lord Almighty.

"But you ask, 'How are we to return?

"Will a mere mortal rob God? Yet you rob me.

"But you ask, 'How are we robbing you?'

In tithes and offerings. You are under a curse—your whole nation—because you are robbing me. Bring the whole tithe into the storehouse, that there may be food in my house. Test me in this, says the Lord Almighty, and see if I will not throw open the floodgates of heaven and pour out so much blessing that there will not be room enough to store it. I will prevent pests from devouring your crops, and the vines in your fields will not drop their fruit before it is ripe, says the Lord Almighty. Then all the nations will call you blessed, for yours will be a delightful land, says the Lord Almighty (Malachi 3:6–12).

Here is a God longing for a right relationship with His people, with a people drowning in their unwillingness to recognize who and what He is, failing to understand what He could be doing for them if they were not frustrating His blessings at every turn.

Our God seen in the Old Testament interacts more like a judge than a loving Father. This sternness results from the disrespect and disobedience His chosen people have shown Him over centuries and particularly evident at the time this book of the Bible is being communicated.

He accuses them of robbing Him of more than any misapplied funds or offerings that should be coming to Him. He is not a God in need. Rather, He expresses His profound love and ultimate disappointment in their actions, "robbing" Him of His ability and opportunity to bless them!

He is God. He needs nothing from them. What He wants is the same kind of relationship with His people that He enjoyed with Adam and Eve before the Fall, when they depended on Him for everything, and He gladly provided it. Their lack of turning to Him in dependence, their corruption, and their disrespect rob Him of the opportunity that He wants most: a relationship founded on their faith in Him where He could bless them mightily.

Points To Consider:

This passage of Malachi 3:6–12 is the crux and the impetus for this book. A depressed people, unfocused on God, have by their selfishness and self-absorption denied God the opportunity to bless them.

In spite of their self-centeredness, He offers them a deal—not for His benefit but for theirs. He loves them so much that He is willing to forego His privilege as the Supreme Being and reach down to them at their level. This love will further be shown centuries later as He gives His Son to obtain a path to a right relationship between God and man.

"Test me in this," says the Lord Almighty.

The Message of Malachi 3

This passage is full of lessons to be learned. Among them:

God does not change. God instituted tithing before the Levitical law, arguably all the way back to Cain and Abel when only four people were on the Earth. God accepted tithing then. God accepted tithing throughout the Old Testament when Abraham tithed to Melchizedek before Levitical law and after the Levitical law was established.

In the Old Testament, God considered not tithing to be robbing Him. That doesn't mean taking His gold and money. He invented money, and the streets in heaven are paved in gold. He doesn't need your money.

No, the robbery takes place when people don't tithe. It robs God of a way to supernaturally bless you. Tithing is a supernatural experience that stems from our faith in God and allows us to partake in God's wonderful reward. From His grace to us by faith, you are blessed by depending on God.

Am I saying I, along with my wife and family, have been supernaturally blessed? That is exactly what I am saying. Finances are only a part of it; our marriage, our children, our grandchildren—everything that has happened in the last 30 years has been led by God or orchestrated to our benefit by tithing and faith in Him.

Have we had struggles and conflicts to contend with? Of course but the overall trajectory of our family has been ascending since we began to tithe. Included in the blessings have been greater peace, based largely on seeing Him work in our lives, and a tremendous sense of well-being that comes from knowing He is near.

There is no explanation other than God playing out this verse in our lives.

He has made this grace available to all. We are gladly taking as much of it as our faith will allow. Lord, increase my faith! May we see your grace even more in our lives!

By the way, you should personalize that last paragraph yourself. I pray God's grace will bless you mightily as well.

Think of this also: This is the last scripture to be written for 460 years. The next scripture contains the Gospels and the New Testament. He sent Malachi and then kept quiet for five centuries. I think it means a lot to Him.

Finally, let's compare this passage to the New Testament standard of giving announced by Paul: "Every man according as he purposeth in his heart, so let him give; not grudgingly, or of necessity: for God loveth a cheerful giver" (2 Corinthians 9:7 KJV).

Points To Consider:

The Law was a hard way to live. The Law was in place to show people that they could not live up to it. The Law pointed the way to the need for a Savior.

Hallelujah! The Savior came, He satisfied the Law and God's perfect justice, and now, we can live in a freer existence with direct access to our Savior and the Trinity!

The emphasis is not on obeying rules but maintaining and deepening a right relationship with the Godhead, like it was intended in the Garden and what Jesus died for so that the object of God's love could be returned to fellowship with Him.

God could not relate to imperfect man directly, which is why Melchizedek approached Abraham and even Moses could only see where God had been, for no man could see His face and live.

Now, with a relationship established through the Son, a relationship of love, the emphasis is not on rule following but staying in fellowship and enjoying all the benefits fellowship brings.

Even in our giving, God has relaxed His expectations, but that said, try to find a verse in the New Testament where giving did not exceed tithing. You won't find it.

God changes not. He still supernaturally blesses the one who by faith gives a tenth of his money willingly, knowing by faith that God will fulfill His promises to bless such an act.

Faith is the currency of Heaven. If you want to get God revved up to act on your behalf, exercise your faith by tithing. Test Him in this!

Tithing was required in the Old Testament because the tithe supported both the civil and religious governance of Israel, the client-state to God. It had a broader coverage than tithing today.

Still, the religious aspects of tithing promised blessing.

Can you see ways in which God would bless one who tithes in today's world? Do you believe God's promise to the Jews, 2,500 years ago, could be a blessing to you?

Are we required to tithe? Are we promised blessings if we tithe?

Do those blessings from tithing today come from faith or abiding the Law?

God used Malachi and Ezra to chastise and exhort the Jews into reflection on God and His desires. Nehemiah, a man of God serving as the chief civil leader, restored the nation by emphasizing God's place in their lives and livelihood. Following God spurred the Nation into prosperity, just like He said He would in the Book of Malachi. Could a population dedicated to serving God bring blessings to our nation as well? How?

Malachi and Me

"Bring the whole tithe into the storehouse, that there may be food in my house. Test me in this," says the LORD Almighty, "and see if I will not throw open the floodgates of heaven and pour out so much blessing that there will not be room enough to store it."

—*Malachi 3:10*

After He chastised the Israelites for their lack of faith and following the pattern of worship laid down in the Levitical law, He offers them a deal.

Think of that. God is offering them the opportunity to put Him to the test. In Matthew 4:7, Jesus says this when he is in conversation with Satan: "Jesus answered him, 'It is also written: 'Do not put the

LORD your God to the test.'" Deuteronomy 6:16 reads: "Do not put the LORD your God to the test as you did at Massah." In context, this serves as a warning against challenging or doubting God's power or promises. Yet here in Malachi, God makes an exception. This act of worship and faith means so much to Him that He is willing to let people test Him so that His supernatural grace can be released fully upon those who believe and act on His promise.

So, if God the Father is offering these slackers and sinful people an opportunity to put Him to a test, it must be a pretty big deal. While we're at it, He is offering the same deal to us, even now!

God is telling you to put Him to the test and see if He doesn't do every bit of what He promises in this verse: Malachi 3:10. This one verse turned my life around.

At a time when I was financially in a helpless situation with dire consequences—I mean dire consequences—looming, I took the sovereign God at His word by faith and started tithing, He did everything He promised in this verse and more. He did this "Exceedingly abundantly above all that we ask or think" (Ephesians 3:20 KJV).

He has continued to honor that promise, specifically to me, for nearly 30 years. Since He does not show favoritism, He is ready to do the same for you.

Points To Consider:

This promise remains and is available to you.

"For it is by grace you have been saved, through faith—and this is not from yourselves, it is the gift of God—not by works, so that no one can boast." Ephesians 2:8–9

This passage applies to both eternal *and* financial salvation. Faith is the key that unlocks the blessing.

An Aside About the Law and Grace

Jesus has fulfilled all the commandments, all the time for you, even paying your penalty for breaking them. In essence, in the Old Testament, people served God. People in the Old Testament had to work to receive the benefits: do good, get good. Old Testament believers were under obedience to the Law to get benefits. Now, since the cross, God serves the believer.

What do I mean by that last sentence? The cross allows God to bestow all His love on us because we, as believers, are back in right relationship with Him. He wants us to believe in His gift—Jesus—and to depend on Him daily in and by faith. You are now obedient to the faith in Jesus Christ and Him crucified. Jesus did the work of eliminating the sin barrier between God the Father and man. You are the beneficiary daily by believing in faith in His finished work. That finished work provides for our salvation, and in His resurrection, He reclaimed the keys to Heaven and Earth. All power is in Him, and He loves you the most!

"It is finished," He said with His last breath on Earth (John 19:30). Now, by faith, you are blessed to enjoy all the loving work He accomplished while here and, even more, all the blessings His resurrection has made available. Satan and death are defeated, sin no longer separates a believer from God, we have access to a loving Father through the Son, and the Holy Spirit is there for us every minute of every day.

Glory to God! Thank you, Jesus!

Why do you worry? The God of the universe is real, and you are His favorite. His love is overwhelming. The only limit to His power working in your life is your faith.

This is where the New Testament separates from the Old Testament. The Old Testament required effort to comply with the Law. The New Testament requires faith in the finished work of Jesus.

Faith, not works, is the finished work of the New Testament. You should live in the New Testament age as obedient to the faith in God's grace, Jesus, full of grace and truth (John 1:14).

Points To Consider:

> **God wants you to have faith in Him as a loving Father who desires a right relationship with His child.**
>
> **Faith in Him and His love for you and faith in the sacrifice of His Son, who made a right relationship possible between man and God, are the essentials of a blessed life and fantastic eternity!**

The Law didn't save but rather pointed out the need for a Savior. "Why, then, was the law given? It was given alongside the promise to show people their sins. But the law was designed to last only until the coming of the child who was promised. God gave his Law through angels to Moses, who was the mediator between God and the people" (Galatians 3:19 NLT). Indeed, while not providing salvation, it was instrumental in making humankind aware of how far short of righteousness they had fallen. "Therefore no one will be declared righteous in God's sight by the works of the law; rather, through the law we become conscious of our sins" (Romans 3:20).

The Law was good and holy (Romans 7:12), but it did not save the nation of Israel and set them free from sin. A Savior—Jesus—was needed for that justification and forgiveness. "Therefore, my friends, I want you to know that through Jesus the forgiveness of sins is proclaimed to you. Through him everyone who believes is set free from every sin, a justification you were not able to obtain under the law of Moses" (Acts 13:38–39).

It points the way to blessing, but no one, save one man, Jesus Christ our Savior, kept the Law perfectly throughout His lifetime.

Jesus took the sins of the world, past, present, and future on His body at the cross. As a believer in His status as fully God yet fully man (hypostatic union, and why He was born unto a virgin), you also know of His giving up the powers of deity while on the earth, save the powers of faith and prayer. Living on Earth led to Him being the perfect man, the only person capable of being the sacrifice for all sins of all people for all time. This perfect life made Him the only one eligible as the sacrifice for our sins.

He completely fulfilled the Law without sinning and paid the price each of us should pay for our sins. When we believe in Him and His finished work on the cross, we are identified with Christ, immediately indwelt by the Holy Spirit, receive eternal life (once saved, always saved), and when we sin, we are no longer condemned to Hell because that price was already paid in full.

There might be other consequences (jail, civil penalties, divorce, estrangement from others), but eternal separation from God is not one of them. That price has been paid for by the precious blood of the Lamb. PRAISE GOD!

Point To Consider:

God can't pour into a clenched fist.

PART II

Christ on Earth

Prophecies About the Coming King

Balaam and the Magi

Around 1446 BC, the Israelites, God's chosen people, left Egypt. Sometime early in the sojourn, God had them go against the giants, the Anakites at what is now Hebron. Twelve spies went in. They all marveled at the land but 10 of the spies came back with a negative report. Only two, Joshua and Caleb, advised going in and taking the land. The other 10 argued the giants were too strong and that they felt like "grasshoppers in our own eyes" (Numbers 13:33). This caused God to send them on a forty-year march, until all people over 20 at the time of the report (except Joshua and Caleb) had died. Then, the people (the younger generation) obeyed God and first took Jericho (all obeying except Achan). Then, they began successful quests of all the cities in their path as they subdued the Promised Land.

In Numbers 22–24, we meet Balaam, an Arab son of Abraham through Ishmael. Ishmael was a *Magos*, (which in the plural is Magi). He is the greedy prophet whose donkey tried to deter him from cursing Israel (Numbers 22–24). His greed caused him to look for a way to curse Israel, which eventually led to his violent death. Before this takes place, he makes a prophetic pronouncement that will be fulfilled centuries later. Speaking of Jesus, he says in Numbers 24:17: "I see him, but not now; I behold him, but not near. A star will come out of Jacob; A scepter will rise out of Israel."

This pronouncement led groups of Magi to look toward the stars for centuries to find when and where the Savior would be born. They were also the wise men saved by Daniel from Nebuchadnezzar's wrath in Daniel 2:24 and who no doubt learned from Daniel about the forthcoming King in the years to come. Imagine their excitement when the prophecy and the sky united to show them the way!

Coming from Persia to Jerusalem and then Bethlehem was about a thousand-mile journey. They were amply provisioned, including chests of treasures to get them there and back, and gifts to honor the Savior, including gold, frankincense, and myrrh.

These three gifts have led people to believe there were only three kings. I, too, like singing the song over the holidays, but unfortunately, the three gifts do not give a true assessment of the expedition of kings and their support staff for such a trip for royalty over two thousand years ago. They were likely a caravan of important people and their helpers making the trip and likely more than three kings or high dignitaries. The gifts may have been only three, but the group was larger, likely riding on Arabian horses with amply supported staff for the long trek.

They were not there at the nativity. As an aside, Jesus was born in a manger, the place where sacrificial lambs were born on their way to their ultimate destination (coincidence? I don't think so). The Bible mentions the "young child" so not a baby. It also mentions they met Jesus at a house, not a stable. It wasn't by accident that Herod the Great killed all the children of Bethlehem under two years old. Communication of news took a long time in those days.

Here is what is important regarding the Magi in this context: the Magi were rich, amply supplied, and focused on the Savior. They traveled for months across a difficult land. They were held in high enough esteem to meet with King Herod, who deferred to them and wished them success on their journey, albeit for his own purposes to eventually kill the child.

> When they saw the star, they were overjoyed. On coming to the house, they saw the child with his mother Mary, and they bowed down and worshiped him. Then they opened their treasures and presented him with gifts of gold, frankincense and myrrh (Matthew 2:10–11).

Read this again closely. When they encountered the King of the Jews, they were overjoyed, and they gave out of their joy. Further, consider the gifts: Gold is the metal of kings, and frankincense was added to offerings by Jews and signified God's satisfaction with the gift, a sweet savor. But what of myrrh?

Myrrh was used for preserving dead people. Jesus was packed in one hundred pounds of myrrh after His crucifixion. The Magi giving Jesus myrrh would be like giving a toddler a casket. This signified that this babe was born to be King, the babe was pleasing to God, and ultimately, the child was to die for all.

On a more cheerful note, consider this: encountering Christ brings joy, and joy brings giving. Giving also brings joy.

Matthew 2:1–2 speaks of The Joyous Kings—the wise men who came to Jerusalem. Verse 9 describes the star that led them until they came to the house (not the stable). The passage also speaks of a thousand-mile, six–nine-month journey, to see a "young child."

Balaam's prophecy foretold a star that would herald the birth of the King of the Jews. A star went before them. A star stopped over the house.

Micah 5:2 tells us the child was to be born in Bethlehem. Exceedingly great joy was to be part of Christmas! They fell and worshipped a toddler. They worshipped exuberantly and opened their treasures—including their money to get there and back—and then, when they met the Savior, they gave to Him extravagantly.

Before they met the Savior, they needed other people to tell them where He was born. After they gave their gifts, God spoke directly to them, warning them not to return to Herod.

You want God to speak to you? Be an extravagant worshipper and an extravagant giver. You want to have joy? Do both. Let yourself go. If you are selfish, you will never have joy.

As mentioned above, Herod ordered the slaughter of all the two-and-under male babies to ensure he had killed the future King. Joseph, warned by an angel, escaped with Mary and Jesus before the slaughter. How did this massacre work out for Herod? Matthew 2:16, 19: Five days after he killed the babies, intent on keeping the kingship for himself, Herod failed horribly and died in excruciating pain.

What will attack joy more than anything is trying to stay in control. Trying to hold on is not the spirit of the wise men but of Herod. Letting go and letting God bloom in your life brings overwhelming joy, especially in giving. Give up control to the God of the universe. Experience the joy of the Magi giving to God.

POINTS TO CONSIDER:

How can you promote your life blooming to the glory of God?

How does tithing promote blooming to the glory of God?

What role does faith have in your life blooming to the glory of God?

Does faith evidenced by giving bring joy?

Read 2 Corinthians 9:7

Introduction to Tithing in the New Testament

How did Christ's incarnation, death, and resurrection change things for humanity? Further, what is the right place for tithing in a grace-oriented time, as opposed to the time of the Law?

One of the great joys of living in Christ's sacrifice for all on the cross is that changed relationship we have with God. No longer do we deal with God as the judge, based on the Law. Now, we are blessed with a relationship with God the Father, who sent His Son to fulfill the Law and provide us with a right relationship with the Trinity through His grace in dying for our sins on the cross. Christ went to hell for three days to regain the keys of dominion over the world (Revelation 1:18) and now sits at the right hand of God the Father for eternity.

Based on the saving grace of Christ, God the judge is now free to deal with us as a loving Father. Our sins are forgiven because when we accept Christ, we are identified with Christ. When we sin, we are no longer judged by that sin but by our identity in Christ. We are sons and daughters in the family of God.

Christ came to fulfill the Law perfectly and to provide us with a path to salvation. That path is part of God's grace to us. No longer is the administration of God's relationship with humankind based on the Law. Our relationship is post-Law. The sin barrier has been removed by Christ's death and resurrection on the cross. Our relationship with God is now based upon and administered under God's grace.

The Word became flesh and made his dwelling among us. We have seen his glory, the glory of the one and only Son, who came from the Father, full of grace and truth.

—John 1:14

Think of how wonderful it is having God's grace at the center of your relationship with Him. The God who created Adam and Eve, only to see them fall, now has an avenue to bless us in every aspect of our lives. He knows we are unable not to sin but has provided us the means (believing in Jesus' death and resurrection) to move past sin in our relationship with Him. Confess your sin and keep moving on with Him. Sin is no longer a barrier to a daily, minute-by-minute walk with Him.

In the Old Testament, the Law was the main point of contact between God and man. Perform well in accordance with the Law and God would be pleased, at least until you broke one of the 603 Jewish Laws or any of God's written 10.

Jesus changed all that. He lived a perfect life and in doing so, showed us the way we could access God the Father and live a blessed life in relationship with the Godhead. Sin was defeated, giving God the ability to bless man like He had always wanted.

Grace is like manna in the desert. We each have access to as much or as little as we need for one day, the day we are living today. Christ Jesus makes it available, in whatever from we need.

Faith is the key to accessing this grace, taking as much grace as the situation requires:

- For salvation: "For it is by grace you have been saved, through faith—and this is not from yourselves, it is the gift of God—not by works, so that no one can boast" (Ephesians 2:8–9).

- For peace and hope: "Therefore, since we have been justified through faith, we have peace with God through our Lord Jesus Christ, through whom we have gained access by faith into this grace in which we now stand. And we boast in the hope of the glory of God" (Romans 5:1–2).

In the Old Testament, our righteousness was administered by adherence to laws written on stone. Now, in the New Testament, we have the Holy Spirit, the Spirit that dwells in us the moment we believe and accept the salvation Jesus provided us on the cross. Thereafter, our fruit from the Spirit (Galatians 5:22–23) is, "…love, joy, peace, forbearance, kindness, goodness, faithfulness, gentleness and self-control. Against such things there is no law." Through the Holy Spirit, our fruit is manifested. Morality isn't from rules but is governed by the Holy Spirit and our yielding to the guidance the Holy Spirit provides. Yielding to Him modifies our conduct and asking Him in prayer for guidance daily, constantly (praying without ceasing), will result in His showing you the right path and His will for your life. The rules are not so much for what is written on stone tablets but what is written on your heart in adherence to the guidance of the Holy Spirit, our administrator, if we let Him. Praying without ceasing will increase your reliance on Him, and since the Spirit is part of the Holy Trinity (Father, Son, and Holy Spirit), you will become more attuned to His guidance, which will lead you from wrong conduct, protect you from bad situations, and provide you the grace you need daily and at critical moments. Develop an ongoing conversation with the Holy Spirit and see how your life changes.

Among other things, you will find destructive behavior less appealing. You might find taking recreational drugs to be less pleasurable because the Holy Spirit is your new best friend. You might avoid signing bad agreements because the voice inside of you is not giving you peace about a situation. You might get prompts to go another way, either to avoid an accident or to find that new breakfast place you have wanted to try. The Holy Spirit's promptings are not all about things dire but can lead you into a generally better life. Old, destructive habits will likely lose some appeal and when your homies begin to say you aren't the same anymore, you can reflect, "thank God." Living in the Spirit is just a better way to live.

He has made us competent as ministers of a new covenant—not of the letter but of the Spirit; for the letter kills, but the Spirit gives life.

—2 Corinthians 3:6

Grace, which is Christ Jesus "The Word became flesh and made his dwelling among us. We have seen his glory, the glory of the one and only Son, who came from the Father, full of grace and truth" (John 1:14:), makes all that we need available, in whatever form we need. Our faith in His grace takes what and how much we need in any circumstance. Faith is the key to accessing God's grace to the full.

Think of it another way: Old Testament believers worked for God. Self-effort was required. Now, God works for us, and by faith, we access what we need in any situation. His grace is amazing!

Other Thoughts on Grace

There are many attributes to God (omniscience, omnipresence, and omnipotence, among others), but here, the discussion centers on God's perfect, infinite love and His perfect, infinite justice.

Before Christ came to live as a human, God's infinite love was restrained by God's infinite justice. Something had to be done to satisfy God's justice because, "the wages of sin is death" (Romans 6:23).

Jesus Christ became that sacrifice, that atonement, that grace which satisfied God's perfect justice and provided the bridge between God and man. "But God demonstrates his own love for us in this: While we were still sinners, Christ died for us" (Romans 5:8). Glory to God!

God must always act first before we can act on behalf of God. He empowers you. God loved you first, which empowered you to love Him. He has enabled you to do good works through His love. "For if, while we were God's enemies, we were reconciled to him through the death of his Son, how much more, having been reconciled, shall we be saved through his life!" (Romans 5:10).

God Himself had to supply what was needed to satisfy His own justice, and that is what happened on the cross. Now, we relate to a God who has unrestrained love for us, given the death that satisfied God's justice forever. This is available for anyone, even the worst person on Earth. "This is love: not that we loved God, but that He loved us and sent his Son as an atoning sacrifice for our sins" (1 John 4:10).

What separated you from God was your sinful nature. That nature was changed when you accept Christ as your Savior. Do you still sin? Sure. There are vestiges of your old self. But now, the Holy Spirit is working in you to align your thoughts and actions to your new nature, one in accordance with God's grace. "He is the one who took God's wrath against our sins upon himself and brought us into fellowship with God; and he is the forgiveness for our sins, and not only ours but all the world's" (1 John 2:2 TLB).

> *"And if by grace, then it cannot be based on works; if it were, grace would no longer be grace."*
>
> —*Romans 11:6*

POINTS TO CONSIDER:

How does faith bring us closer to God than the Law?

Why does God's grace provide us a better channel to relationship with God than the Law?

Does God's gift of His Son for a "right relationship" with you cause you to reflect on your relationship with God?

How Do We Learn From the New Testament?

The books of Matthew, Mark, Luke, and John tell us of the good news of Jesus Christ incarnate. Living as a human being on Earth, Jesus shows the movement away from the edicts of the Law into an emphasis on the good news: the gospel of the grace of God. With His time as a human on Earth, our relationship with the Father, Son, and Holy Spirit changes from one founded on obedience to one based on grace and our newly given ability to access that grace by faith.

How do we learn about faith? "Faith comes by hearing, and hearing by the Word of God" (Romans 10:17 NKJV). Jesus' whole life on Earth was an exercise in grace so that people could see God's love in action, while differentiating the new system from the Old Testament, a system based on obedience that was ultimately impossible to fully follow (unless you were Christ).

The books of the Bible that follow the book of John tell us about the gospel of the grace of God. Whereas Old Testament believers strived to live through self-effort that pleased God, God, after Christ's sacrifice for all on the cross and His resurrection, made it possible to access God's magnificent grace for our eternal lives, tomorrow morning, or even five seconds from now.

God demanded obedience in the Old Testament; now, we are freed from the debt of sin and, through faith, can experience the whole spectrum of His grace, mercy, and blessings. In essence, we believe, and He provides everything else.

What does He provide? Salvation and eternal life in heaven to start. In our daily lives, healing, guidance, strength to rise when you are knocked down, clarity as to how to proceed when you are floundering, and resolve when you are depending on Him.

The Christian life is a personal relationship with Him. By believing in Him, you have been set free; a connection with Him has been formed. With God at your side, providing guidance and wisdom through the Holy Spirit, you can straighten yourself up and excel.

You do this by faith and communicating with Him through prayer. Align yourself with His word by reading His word, His precious food to strengthen and guide us. His word is alive and powerful (Hebrews 4:12)!

He will never leave you nor forsake you. When you are walking with Jesus, like Peter walking on the water, keep your focus on Him. If you lose focus, like Peter, He is always right there to pick you up, just like Jesus did with Peter when he sank. Remember this: Jesus didn't forsake Peter when he was sinking but walked on water over to him, lifted him up, and together they walked to the shore. God is so good!

Stay in faith and live in His grace. When you fail, as you will, confess and get back on track. This is a love relationship, and the hope is to quickly realign yourself to a right relationship with God. Jesus never fails.

Points To Consider:

Does God reward self-effort or faith?

God knows who we are and loves us anyway. What really gets Him moving on our behalf is our demonstrating how much we rely on Him. Reliance on Him is faith. Reliance on our self-effort honors us, and He knows us too well to be impressed. He knows the best looking, smartest, most powerful person ever born started out as dust.

It has been said that "faith is the currency of Heaven." What does that mean and how does it apply to our relationship with God?

Consider these four passages:

Matthew 9:2: "Some men brought to him a paralyzed man, lying on a mat. When Jesus saw their faith, he said to the man, 'Take heart, son; your sins are forgiven.'"

Matthew 9:22: "Jesus turned and saw her. 'Take heart, daughter,' he said, 'your faith has healed you.' And the woman was healed at that moment."

Matthew 9:29: "Then he touched their eyes and said, 'According to your faith let it be done to you.'"

Matthew 15:28: "Then Jesus said to her, 'Woman, you have great faith! Your request is granted.' And her daughter was healed at that moment."

Jesus healed a paralyzed man, a sick woman, two blind men, and a demon-possessed girl in these quoted passages, all as a result in their faith in Him. Faith brings God into action, not exclusively, but clearly and often miraculously.

Old Testament Law & New Testament Grace

The Law was given specifically to the Jews to demonstrate that no fallible being, like humans since the time of Adam, could do anything to live a perfect life. The Law is perfect. We aren't. Some 1,500 years or so later, Jesus was born and lived a perfect life. No one else has ever lived perfectly before or since. That is why only Jesus is worthy of the sacrifice to free us from the penalty of sin and to provide the avenue to a tremendously successful, blessed life.

The Law points the way to the fact that there is no hope in ourselves for salvation. No one was worthy as the sacrifice, "for all have sinned and fall short of the glory of God" (Romans 3:23). As such, we needed and need now, a Savior.

That Savior is Jesus Christ. He came for salvation. He also came to show us the way to live an outstanding, blessed life by following the promptings and guidance of the Holy Spirit (be sensitive to the Holy Spirit in your life for you should depend on God always, every day). That is faith at its best. Faith offers your best life by staying in right relationship with God. Ultimately, God sent His son Jesus to die for us because he wanted a love-filled relationship with the likes of you and me. Again, Praise God!

How does this work? Some of the greatest humans that have ever lived—Abraham, Moses, David, any Old Testament greats—realized their sinfulness. All the Old Testament heroes of Hebrews 11 did admirable things, but they were missing the empowerment of the Holy Spirit.

The Holy Spirit teaches us how to live, prompts us to do right in our daily life, warns us about the course we are taking, puts us back on the right path when we sin, and strengthens us to learn righteousness as we get on with our daily lives. The Holy Spirit shows us the better way, making sin so much less attractive than it was before the indwelling of the Holy Spirit. The Holy Spirit gives us life and gives it to us more abundantly (John 10:10).

The Law was never designed to do that. Jesus was always the source of creation and of life. Jesus provides life to us through our faith in Him, empowers us through the Holy Spirit to align our lives towards God's plan for our lives and to please Him increasingly each day as we grow in our relationship with Him.

In the Old Testament, compliance with the Jewish Law stemmed from fear, not only of punishment but of lost blessings. You needed to do good to receive good. God blessed those who followed the Law and did not bless those who did not follow the Law. In essence, the Law limited God's ability to show His love to the Jews because of their actions.

In the New Testament, the whole weight of sin and its destructiveness was put on Jesus. Now, because Jesus has paid the price (as Bill Maher once said: "talk about picking up the tab for the whole table!"), God is no longer limited by our imperfections in blessing us. When God sees the New Testament believer, He sees Christ in us.

93

Sin is no longer the issue because it has been paid for. Dad doesn't sweat sin anymore.

Our relationship with God can flourish because we are no longer separated. You still sin occasionally, but you are blessed by Jesus' work on the cross and can get right with God quickly: "If we confess our sins, He is faithful and just to forgive us our sins…"(1 John 1:9 KJV). While beginning to walk, stay on the path and, out of love for God, try to cut down on the stumbles. Confess to cleanse yourself from all unrighteousness and keep moving. Like the child who stumbles when walking with his dad, our Father doesn't want to punish but wants to see you do better next time.

So, how does this relate to tithing now and tithing under the Law?

God commanded the Jews under the Law to tithe. For you, tithing is an option. Old Testament people had no option and faced civil penalties if they didn't, not to mention, God's wrath. They really didn't have a choice. If you don't tithe as a New Testament believer though, you are missing out on promised blessings from God. You can be supernaturally blessed by God or pass on God's promise of blessing to you. The key is faith in God's word. Do you believe Him or not? His promise to bless your tithing is as strong as His pronouncements in the Ten Commandments. Follow it by faith and you can't help but be supernaturally blessed.

Points To Consider:

Don't have a fear consciousness. Be aligned with Christ, righteous for what He has done for you and what He does daily. Believe, receive, rest in His word and instruction. He loves you most of all.

I am righteous for what Jesus has done for me and my belief in what He has said and done. Sin is no longer the issue for a born-again believer.

Look at yourself the way God looks at you as a born-again believer. Why, you look just like Christ!

As to tithing, the promise of Malachi 3:10 is still there for you to accept by faith. New Testament believers are under no compulsion to tithe. Avoid legalism if you do tithe. Still, even though you don't have to, God hasn't voided the promised blessings.

Several Points on New Testament Tithing

New Testament believers do not live under the Law, but it can be reasonably inferred that giving tithe is our reasonable service. The Law codified tithing, a system of honoring God that existed maybe 2,500 years before the Law and certainly 500 years before the Law.

Consider this: God invented money and our economic system. God doesn't need our money. He could create money or gold or jewels whenever He needs. What giving money does is provide us with an opportunity to be blessed by Him. (Malachi 3:8–9)

Though God does not demand tithe from us by law, as New Testament believers, you can be sure the above scripture has not been repealed, and it is as relevant to you as it was to the Jewish shepherd in Goshen.

God designates where the tithe is to be given, the house of God, your local church. Your job is to give and that will be the standard by which you will be judged. How it is properly used to God's glory is the purview of the church and its anointed, who will be judged by God as to how it is spent.

Think of this: The tithe was for everything from the land. God provided every ability for the land to prosper and provide—sun, rain, fertile soil, a growing season for various crops. He was and is the source. Yet, He only asked for a tenth in recognition of His work in the process.

The point is, even though tithing is not demanded in the New Testament, it is still an act of worship, and it is holy to Him. Finally, let's compare this passage to the New Testament standard of giving announced by Paul.

Jesus Fulfilled the Law

Jesus fulfilled the Law and introduced a relationship based on grace and truth because Jesus is grace and truth (John 1:14). But it does not necessarily follow that there aren't aspects of the Old Testament that can be useful to a New Testament believer. Dietary laws, in many cases, are helpful even now. Solomon's wisdom has proven to be a great guide for living over several millennia. The Ten Commandments, the moral guide of the Old Testament, are still to be followed and have not been abrogated. What this book is ultimately about is that yes, you as a New Testament believer are free to make your own way as it applies to tithing and giving. Unfortunately, many people believe that the proper way to live is to live worried while tightly grasping their wallet. They are not living cheerfully; they are living grudgingly. That way of living limits God and does not exhibit faith. That way of living denies the continuing power of Malachi 3:10, which is still available to New Testament people today. God showed us the way to be blessed in our giving in Malachi 3. You aren't required as a New Testament believer to follow it. But I am writing to tell you that every word in Malachi 3:6–10 is the truth, both then and now. I know this because my family and I have been blessed by this scripture for nearly 30 years. God is no respecter of persons (Acts 10:34 KJV). I am no big deal that God would want to honor me especially. This avenue of blessing is available, indeed promised, to you.

In the Old Testament book of Malachi, God got extremely disappointed in the Jews returning from Babylon. They started strong upon their return to the Promised Land but quickly lost focus on God and focused largely on themselves. Worse, the downward spiral of their conduct was coming close to a new low, near equal to the conduct that led to the diaspora (dispersing the Jews from their homeland). They are sullen and again making God a lesser priority. God is frustrated. They are His chosen people, and they are acting displeasingly!

So, what does He do? He says, let's make a deal: You tithe and see if I don't bless you. He says it better than that in Malachi 3:10: "'Bring the whole tithe into the storehouse, that there may be food in my house. Test me in this,' says the LORD Almighty, 'and see if I will not throw open the floodgates of heaven and pour out so much blessing that there will not be room enough to store it.'"

Think of this verse and ask yourself: Did God love these people more than He loves me? If He did, then why did I live to know about Jesus and His sacrifice for me and they did not?

God's timing and His words are perfect. He has never taken away the blessing that comes from the tithe, even though He took away the requirement to tithe found in the Old Testament. You don't live under the Law where compliance with the tithe was mandatory. No, for you, God has given a choice to participate in this blessing or not. It is not a foul if you don't comply, but it is a loss to you if you ignore this promise at your choosing. The key to tithing now is faith: I take you at your word, Lord, that I will be blessed in tithing. I don't know if it is through finances, health, improved family relations, having children, passing that test, kicking a bad habit, or winning the lottery (okay, that smacks very close to the prosperity doctrine, but it still could happen. Please, don't start tithing if your purpose is solely to win the lottery).

God knows you, and tithing pleases Him. He will provide you a blessing, probably many blessings, in some form, at some time, if you give from your faith in Him and His word, not necessarily from the sensibilities of a six year-old at Christmas chanting "Me, me, me!" Do this in faith and gratitude, not from a selfish heart. His word is true.

Points To Consider:

Tithing is no more legalism than washing your hands before eating. It isn't a sin if you don't, but it is still a good idea.

Tithing requires effort but that effort is backed up by faith in a continuing promise that goes back four thousand years. The blessings from tithing still remain.

When Jesus Lived on Earth in Human Form

From Jesus' birth to the cross and His resurrection is the transition period from when the Law ruled the world and grace became the operating system for our relationship to God.

To be worthy as the Lamb, His life had to be lived perfectly, which it was. His death fulfilled the sacrifice needed to restore humankind to God. His journey into hell for the three days before His resurrection restored the keys of the Kingdom of Heaven to the Christ, the keys that Adam had surrendered with the Fall of man after being given those keys in the Garden (Revelation 1:18).

Then God said, Let us make mankind in our image, in our likeness:
and let them have dominion over the fish of the sea, and over the
fowl of the air, and over the cattle, and over all the earth, and over
every creeping thing that creepeth upon the earth

—Genesis 1:26 KJV

God gave dominion to Adam, but when Adam sinned, he surrendered the keys to Satan.

> *[Satan speaking to Jesus in the desert] And I will give you the keys of the kingdom of heaven, and whatever you bind on earth will be bound in heaven, and whatever you loose on earth will be loosed in heaven.*
>
> —*Matthew 16:19 NKJV*

Satan had become the ruler of the Earth with Adam's fall, and Jesus could have accepted Satan's offer, and we all would have been doomed forever. There was no one warming up in the bullpen.

> *[As Jesus said] I am the Living One; I was dead, and now look, I am alive for ever and ever! And I hold the keys of death and Hades.*
>
> —*Revelation 1:18*

Jesus overcame the powers of Satan and sin on the cross, giving us the opportunity for a forgiven life and eternal life with God. The keys to the Kingdom of Heaven were restored to the Savior. As a result, this life could be "exceedingly abundantly above all that we ask or think" by living a life "according to the power that worketh inside of us." (Ephesians 3:20 KJV) That power is faith in God's love:

> *For in Jesus Christ neither circumcision availeth any thing, nor uncircumcision; but faith which worketh by love.*
>
> —*Galatians 5:6 KJV*

Faith, specifically faith in God's love, gets God to move on your behalf. "…Was my arm too short to deliver you? Do I lack the strength to rescue you? …Because the Sovereign LORD helps me, I will not be disgraced… Let the one who walks in the dark, who has no light, trust in the name of the LORD and rely on their God" (Isaiah 50:2, 7, 10).

God loves it when you depend on Him and turn to Him to lead you even in the darkest time. God has the arm length and strength to uphold you in and through any difficulty. Think and pray often this prayer:

God, praise and glory and thanks to you! I know you love me, and I am depending on you today, this hour and minute, every second, every day. When I am not, prompt me to get back in line with your power. I am depending on you now. Amen.

That is the power that lives inside you.

Points To Consider:

The prayer above reflects God's purpose for providing a way for us to access Him (through His Son Jesus Christ) and to properly show your need for guidance and our desire to be led in fellowship with Him. He loves that!

The Holy Spirit wants to guide us lovingly through our day, every day ("Don't do that, go this way, take a moment and think"). Being sensitive to His guidance is a practice that grows stronger, the more you practice turning things over to Him, especially in your everyday. Perhaps praying before you open your mouth might be a good approach to living life.

God wants that kind of relationship with you. He wants to do exceedingly, abundantly, more than you can ever think to make your life the best. What a great joy it is to be loved by God!

You and Your Faith

You demonstrating your faith in Him makes all the sacrifices of Christ worthwhile to the Godhead. You and your faith, were you the only one to ever live or to ever rely on God by faith, would bless God sufficiently for Him to have sent His Son. Don't underestimate your importance to the Lord. Faith in Him and His love sparks God into action for you, His son or daughter. Faith improves and strengthens your relationship with Him in every aspect of your life. Come boldly to God and ask with confidence. Demonstrate your faith in Him.

Think of Jacob, who spent his early life as a schemer, cheater, and deceiver. Yet, when he finally got serious about changing his life, God came to him. After a night of wrestling with the Angel of God, Jacob still had the audacity to demand the Angel bless him. That morning, he changed from Jacob the trickster to Israel, "contends with God." God blessed him because of his boldness and his belief that he would be blessed despite his past.

God will do the same for you.

So how does all of this relate to tithing? Tithing requires faith. "Humble yourselves, therefore, under God's mighty hand, that he may lift you up in due time" (1 Peter 5:6).

What is the opposite of humble? Arrogant, right? And to me, the most arrogant thing I can think of is for me to think I can do more with one hundred percent of my money than God can do with ten percent of my money and His blessings on the other 90 percent.

What's in it for me if I humble myself to this thinking and give the first ten percent of my increase to him? According to 1 Peter 5:6, you are allowing Him the opportunity to lift you up (elevate, enrich, bless—pick any great description) in due time. The "due time" is the time when you are ready.

One of my favorite passages in the Old Testament is when the Jews are starting their exodus from Egypt to the Promise Land. It reads like this:

> When Pharaoh drew near, the people of Israel lifted up their eyes, and behold, the Egyptians were marching after them, and they feared greatly. And the people of Israel cried out to the Lord. They said to Moses, "Is it because there are no

graves in Egypt that you have taken us away to die in the wilderness? What have you done to us in bringing us out of Egypt? Is not this what we said to you in Egypt: 'Leave us alone that we may serve the Egyptians'? For it would have been better for us to serve the Egyptians than to die in the wilderness." And Moses said to the people, "Fear not, stand firm, and see the salvation of the Lord, which he will work for you today. For the Egyptians whom you see today, you shall never see again. The Lord will fight for you, and you have only to be silent."

The Lord said to Moses, "Why do you cry to me? Tell the people of Israel to go forward. Lift up your staff, and stretch out your hand over the sea and divide it, that the people of Israel may go through the sea on dry ground (Exodus 14:10–16 ESV).

What happened? Moses did as he was told. He took a step, the waters parted, and the Israelites went across on dry land. The Israelites went into the channel as departing slaves and came out as a nation. They went in fear and came out exhilarated and with a new sense of identity (albeit short-lived for the older generation).

Think of John 6:28–29 (KJV): "Then said they unto him, What shall we do, that we might work the works of God? Jesus answered and said unto them, This is the work of God, that ye believe on him whom he hath sent."

What did it take in both of these instances? Faith and obedience to God.

Do you see a similarity to you concerning God's promises and future blessings? He has His eyes on you, and He is going to make things right. Take a step and watch the blessings flow.

Points To Consider:

Can you think of instances in the Old Testament where faith was rewarded or changed the circumstances of the one acting in faith?

Consider these: Moses in Exodus 14:14–22; Deborah in Judges 4:14–16; Abram in Genesis 15:6; David in Psalm 37:5; Solomon in Proverbs 3:5; and Habakkuk 2:4.

Tithing During Jesus' Time on Earth

Jesus lived on Earth under the Old Testament rules. So, what happened with all the rules including tithing? He was not here to break the Law but to fulfill it (Matthew 5:17). The new covenant did not become operative until after His death and resurrection. While living as a man on Earth, He lived as an Old Testament Jew introducing the New Testament of grace.

Think of this as a regular person who dies with a last will and testament. While they are living, the will is of no effect. When that person dies, the will becomes operative. In the case of Jesus, who was grace and truth (John 1:14), grace and truth became our operative system for living with His death.

Still, as to tithing, two citations are often brought up about giving a tenth in the New Testament. They read almost the same:

Woe to you, teachers of the law and Pharisees, you hypocrites! You give a tenth of your spices—mint, dill and cumin. But you have neglected the more important matters of the law—justice, mercy and faithfulness. You should have practiced the latter, without neglecting the former (Matthew 23:23).

Woe to you Pharisees, because you give God a tenth of your mint, rue and all other kinds of garden herbs, but you neglect justice and the love of God. You should have practiced the latter without leaving the former undone (Luke 11:42).

Here Jesus is not criticizing the Pharisees for tithing but for their obsessiveness to the Law and disregarding more important issues like justice, mercy, faithfulness, and love of God. He criticizes their hypocrisy and warns them to practice all the intents of the Law. Their obsession with the minutiae of the Law caused them to miss the major tenets the Law embodied. Ultimately, it demonstrated the need for a Savior because no one could meet the demands of the Law, save one man, the God-man, our Lord Jesus Christ.

What does this mean for New Testament believers? We as New Testament believers are not required to live under the Law, which requires tithing. Indeed, tithing is only mentioned in the New Testament in these two settings. Still, tithing does not negate the righteousness of God. We do well to honor God with a tenth of our increase (it worked out well for Abraham, Moses, and David).

Further, the New Testament doesn't really address abstaining from adultery, murder, or stealing, yet these Old Testament issues are best followed in our society today. Just because things aren't addressed in the New Testament with its emphasis on the Christ doesn't mean you should ignore them.

An important issue should be recognized in this discussion. Think about when Jesus was asked whether a man should get divorced. Jesus responded: "Moses permitted you to divorce your wives because your hearts were hard. But it was not this way in the beginning. I tell you that anyone who divorces his wife, except for sexual immorality, and marries another woman commits adultery" (Matthew 19:8–9).

Why the emphasis of the beginning? Because God wants us back to the state before Adam and Eve sinned. He longs for that relationship they had in the garden, perhaps for millions of years, before Satan gained dominion in the world from deceiving them into intentional sin. Why is this important? Tithing was not necessary in the Garden because worshipping God for all provision was natural with Adam and Eve not needing a law for compulsion. Everything worked from love and the joy to honor God, who provided all blessings. God compelled the giving of the tenth after the Fall to provide an avenue of worship for fallen man.

Remember, God had to sew animal skins together to dress Adam and Eve because they didn't know how to dress themselves (Genesis 3:7). A fig leaf? Please! Our original parents were so disoriented that they needed directions for healthy and safe living, especially after the Fall. Also, take a moment to consider God's grace in the matter of their departure. They had broken a fellowship that impacts many people even now, those who don't know Christ as Savior. Still, despite the cataclysmic betrayal, God still took time to sew animal's skins for them upon their departure, the act of a loving parent. What a wonderful God!

One last thing on the issue of tithing in the New Testament:

> This Melchizedek was king of Salem and priest of God Most High. He met Abraham returning from the defeat of the kings and blessed him, and Abraham gave him a tenth of everything. First, the name Melchizedek means "king of righteousness"; then also, "king of Salem" means "king of peace." Without father or mother, without genealogy, without beginning of days or end of life, resembling the Son of God, he remains a priest forever.
>
> Just think how great he was: Even the patriarch Abraham gave him a tenth of the plunder! Now the law requires the descendants of Levi who become priests to collect a tenth from the people—that is, from their fellow Israelites—even though they also are descended from Abraham. This man, however, did not trace his descent from Levi, yet he collected a tenth from Abraham and blessed him who had the promises. And without doubt the lesser is blessed by the greater. In the one case, the tenth is collected by people who die; but in the other case, by him who is declared to be living. One might even say that Levi, who collects the tenth, paid the tenth through Abraham, because when Melchizedek met Abraham, Levi was still in the body of his ancestor (Hebrews 7:1–10).

This passage reiterates the tenth Abraham gave to Melchizedek in the Old Testament. Melchizedek was a type of Christ and a high priest. Jesus is our high priest, and we too should consider giving Him a tenth of our increase.

New Testament believers are encouraged to tithe but are not compelled to by the Law.

Points To Consider:

Melchizedek acted as the intercessor between God and Abraham. That intercession allowed Abraham to give a tenth of his increase, ultimately, to God. From this gift came great blessings, extending down to Abraham's children to this day.

Do you believe this is available to you?

Jesus on Earth—The Law, Grace, and the Adultress

Jesus Christ, our Lord and Savior, came to the earth at the exact right time.

Philippians 2:6–8: "Who, being in very nature God, did not consider equality with God something to be used to his own advantage; rather, he made himself nothing by taking the very nature of a servant, being made in human likeness. And being found in appearance as a man, he humbled himself by becoming obedient to death—even death on a cross!"

During His life on Earth, He was doing two things: He was perfectly fulfilling the Law, as the only person capable and worthy of fulfilling the Law (for all others had an old sin nature passed down from Adam, thus, the need for a virgin birth). This allowed Him to be the perfect sacrifice to satisfy God's perfect justice.

He was also introducing the new operating system that would create a completely new relationship between God and man, one that had the vibrancy of His relationship with Adam and Eve before the Fall but also introduced a method of dealing with the elephant in the room: the sin barrier and our inability not to sin.

One of the great joys of New Testament living is enjoying all the benefits of Christ's sacrifice for all on the cross. That incredible sacrifice changed our relationship with God. No longer do we deal with God as the judge, based on the Law. Now, we are blessed with a relationship with God the Father, one who sent His Son to fulfill the Law and provide us with a right relationship with the Trinity.

How did that happen? By Jesus' grace in dying for our sins on the cross. From there, He went to Hell (Revelation 1:18) to regain the keys of dominion over the world (lost when Adam and Eve sinned), and He is now sitting at the right hand of God the Father for eternity. God the judge is now free, based on the saving grace of Christ, to deal with us as a loving Father.

Our sins are forgiven because when we accept Christ, we are identified with Christ, the Perfect One. When we sin, we are no longer judged by that sin but by our identity in Christ. We are sons and daughters in the family of God. Christ came to fulfill the Law perfectly and to provide us with a path to salvation. That path is part of God's grace to us. Many of His statements while on Earth reflect His completion of the Old Testament law. In others, He is describing the New Testament age to come and how the world is to operate.

But He was also here to introduce and demonstrate the life we could/would have after His sacrifice on the cross. Christ came to fulfill the Law perfectly and to provide us with a path to salvation. That path is part of God's grace to us.

This transition from a life under the Law and into a life of grace is demonstrated in several instances in Jesus' life in the Gospels, which tell His story while on Earth. Perhaps most clearly, the story of grace replacing the Law is told in the woman caught in adultery who is brought to Jesus.

Points To Consider:

Why is it called Adam's sin if Eve first ate the apple?

Since it was from Adam that we get the old sin nature, is that one of the reasons Jesus needed to be born from a virgin?

How did Jesus' perfect life fulfill the requirements for the sacrifice for all?

Among God's attributes, He is perfect love but also perfect justice. To overcome sin, a perfect lamb had to die to provide the bridge from God to man. Was God's perfect justice satisfied with Jesus' death on the cross?

How are we benefited by the sacrifice of the perfect lamb? See John 1:29; 1 Corinthians 5:7; 1 John 2:2; 1 Peter 1:18–20; Hebrews 9:12.

The Woman Caught in Adultery

Let me give you an example of how Jesus fulfilled the Law in His incarnation but acted in grace throughout His time here.

This example, found in John 8:3–11, might seem a little unusual in a book about tithing, but consider the woman caught in the act of adultery. She is brought to Jesus from the very act of sinning, a sin that under the Law requires death (it should be noted that the man she was with was also required under the Law to die, but the hypocrisy involved here is another story).

The Jewish leaders bring her to Jesus, state the facts of her sin, and ask what should be done to her. The Law clearly states death. Jesus, to fulfill the Law, cannot break the Law and still be the Savior. His answer has large implications not only for the immediate scene but for all of us thereafter. Taking the position to let her go breaks the Mosaic Law. Telling them to stone her defeats the grace of God.

Right here, the Law is confronting grace (Jesus is grace, John 1:14). The operating system of the world (the Law) is facing the new operating system (grace).

So, what does He do?

He says, "He who is without sin cast the first stone."

That stops the crowd. The older people, recognizing they have a whole lot of sins, are the first to drop their stones. Eventually, all the crowd leaves, leaving Jesus and the woman alone.

Here is where the story connects with the purpose of this book: Jesus asks who is left to condemn you? The woman replies "no one." Jesus says, "Neither do I condemn you; go and sin no more" (John 8:11 NKJV).

At that moment, grace supplants the Law. The Law, espoused by the Old Testament scribes, runs straight into the grace of the New Testament world, Jesus, full of grace and truth.

The grace response to the Law—He who is without sin, cast the first stone—thus supersedes the Law and causes them to drift away. The woman, having experienced God's grace at the point of death, is free to move on from her sin and to experience a life in fellowship with God's grace.

There are many other examples during His life on Earth where He exhibits grace while fulfilling the Law: the great faith of the centurion (Matthew 7:1–10); resurrecting the widow's son (Luke 7:11–15); the harlot kissing His feet while He was eating with the Pharisees (Luke 7:36–50).

In every situation, He followed the Law but made room to give grace to those in need.

So, how does grace apply to tithing? As New Testament believers, we have a completely different relationship with God than Moses, David, and all the heroes of the Old Testament mentioned in Hebrews 11.

We tithe, now, not from compulsion of a Law but in our faith in His word. He tells us in Malachi 3:10: "'Bring the whole tithe into the storehouse, that there may be food in my house. Test me in this,' says the LORD Almighty, 'and see if I will not throw open the floodgates of heaven and pour out so much blessing that there will not be room enough to store it.'"

Do I have to do that like an Old Testament Jew? No. Can I do it by faith in my God who has blessed me with salvation, His peace and love, and His solemn word in this scripture?

Yes, I can. Will I receive by faith the same blessings He promises? I will, and I have 30 years of proof in my life. Glory to God! He is so wonderful, and His words are true!

(Between the above paragraph and the following paragraph, I needed to take a moment to praise and worship Him! Glory be to God; every word is true!)

I am not writing this as a thesis or something. I have seen for myself the grace and faithfulness God has bestowed upon me and my family for a right response to this passage. I pray you take it seriously and, by faith, claim it like I did. I promise you every word is good and true and is still applicable to you as a New Testament Christian. Do it by faith!

Okay, back to where I was:

God is our Father. We deal with Him through the saving work of His Son. Sin is no longer the point of contact but through the right relationship to the Father that Jesus' life provided. If we sin, we have 1 John 1:9: "If we confess our sin, He is faithful and just and will forgive us our sins and purify us from all unrighteousness." Our sins are forgiven, that places us in a right relationship with God to access His grace by faith. Glory to God! Thank you, Lord Jesus! Thank you, Holy Spirit!

Points To Consider:

Can you see the difference between the Law and grace?

God isn't seeking retribution for law breaking. He already knows we all are law breakers. The beauty of this story shows the way to a marvelous, grace-filled era that exists even today. You mess up, even big time, and He wants you to get back on track with a loving relationship with Him.

Look at the standard to be applied in 1 John 1:9.

Think about the shock to their system with Jesus' response: The Pharisees were looking to trap Him and He ends up shaking their entire belief system.

The general audience was looking for a diversion (no TV) and ended up having their minds challenged and, likely, with the realization that their lives needed to be modified with this new doctrine.

1,500 years of teaching and tradition were successfully challenged in one confrontation.

The world was beginning to change as God was implementing a new system of relating to humanity.

Jesus As a Man On Earth

Things to think about the incarnate Christ:

Jesus lived His whole life on Earth under the Law. His fulfillment of the Law was crucial to being the perfect lamb, the only worthy sacrifice for all time. His words on the cross, "It is finished," signified the completion of His task in earthly form; He was the sacrifice for all for all time.

The New Testament age did not become effective until after His death and resurrection. Indeed, Pentecost (which means "50") began the church 50 days after His resurrection.

As the Law was completed, one cannot argue that Jesus was requiring tithing into the New Testament. In both Matthew 23 and Luke 11, Jesus was affirming the practice of tithing but only if accompanied by love, justice, and faithfulness, elements not necessarily found in the Old Testament application and obedience.

The early church did not speak much about tithing as non-Jews would find this discussion confusing and outside the central message of salvation.

Yet, consider Jesus talking about divorce in Matthew 19:8: "Jesus replied, 'Moses permitted you to divorce your wives because your hearts were hard. But it was not this way from the beginning….'" Jesus was calling attention to God's original plan—life in the perfect environment of the garden, before the Fall.

The Law revealed God's righteousness, but it only offered condemnation. No one but Jesus could meet the Law's standards every moment, every day. The Law condemned and did not save. Salvation only came through Jesus' death and resurrection, and our identification with Him through faith.

That pure love in the garden was replaced in the Law with rules of conduct compelling actions. The New Testament operates not by compulsion but through love, faith, and God's grace. Like Abraham, our giving a tenth of our income and increase is not compelled but is an appropriate demonstration of the entirety of our relationship with God-love, dependence, worship, reverence, respect, and His awesomeness in every aspect of our lives.

Contrasting the Law and a Spirit Led Grace Life

For I command you today to love the Lord your God, to walk in obedience to him, and to keep his commands, decrees and laws; then you will live and increase, and the Lᴏʀᴅ your God will bless you in the land you are entering to possess.

But if your heart turns away and you are not obedient, and if you are drawn away to bow down to other gods and worship them, I declare to you this day that you will certainly be destroyed. You will not live long in the land you are crossing the Jordan to enter and possess (Deuteronomy 30:16–18).

God gave the Israelites 10 Commandments, and the Israelites added 603 laws to administer those 10 Commandments. These laws were in place to mandate morality. Consider the man picking up sticks on the Sabbath being stoned to death for such an egregious act. Seriously, was that part of God's plan or was it man's interpretation and response?

Either way, the legislation of morality failed miserably. The attempt to get the Commandments to manifest morality in people's lives changed the focus from the intent of the Law to an obsession on the minutiae, quite apart from God's intent.

For the New Testament believer, we have the Holy Spirit to guide and refresh our lives. The Holy Spirit, living inside the believer, inwardly administers our conduct by promptings and insights. The closer attuned you are to the Holy Spirit, the stronger, happier, and more clearheaded and joyful you will be.

The Holy Spirit is God in us. He changes you from the inside. We live by the commandment of love, believing on the one God sent to free us from sin and to thrive in a Spirit led existence.

For it is God who works in you to will and to act in order to fulfill his good purpose.

—Philippians 2:13

The Holy Spirit is working on your desires and actions to do what pleases Him, to bring about a change aligned with His will and purpose.

And he who searches our hearts knows the mind of the Spirit, because the Spirit intercedes for God's people in accordance with the will of God. And we know that in all things God works for the good of those who love him, who have been called according to his purpose.

—Romans 8:27–28

God's love extends to even the worst sinners. His dying on the cross for us resolved the issue of sin for the believer. We are free from the external laws of the Old Testament. We live according to the law of the Spirit. Praise God for that!

Against this backdrop, let's see how this played out during Jesus' time on Earth.

Points To Consider:

What are some of the differences between living under the Law and living under grace as our operating system?

How was the Law enforced? How does grace operate?

What Commandment are we to follow in the New Testament age?

Read 2 John 1:5 and John 6:28–29.

Incarnate Jesus Living Under the Law and Tithing

Between the Old and New Testament, Jesus lived on Earth. The New Testament started with Pentecost, 50 days after the resurrection. That was the day when the Holy Spirit first indwelt believers, all the Jews in Jerusalem heard the Gospel in their own language, and 3,000 people were saved. As mentioned earlier, this is in contrast to when 3,000 Israelites died at the giving of the 10 Commandments.

Among the reasons Jesus came to Earth in human form was to complete the Law. That means that Jesus, the perfect one, was the only person capable of fulfilling the Law, to be the perfect Lamb of God, the sacrifice for all mankind.

God the Father is perfect. As such, God can have nothing to do with imperfection. For Him to associate with the imperfect would be out of His character. Besides, would you want a God that compromised and allowed imperfection as a standard? That would be chaotic and abhorrent on so many levels. God is perfect. He is immutable, and He does not compromise. His perfect justice would not allow that.

As we have discussed, God over the centuries has found reasonable methods to deal with sinful man: Abraham was visited by Melchizedek, a pre-incarnate form of the Savior. Sacrifices of lambs and other livestock over the centuries allowed the animal blood to cover (not cleanse) the sins of man so that God could interact with humans.

Now, with the incarnation of the Lord Jesus Christ, we have God in human form coming to the world to fulfill the Law (He is the only one able to live a sinless life and fulfill the Law perfectly) and to be the perfect Lamb, the sacrifice for all mankind, providing a right relationship with God and eternal salvation. Glory to God!

So how does Jesus' incarnation and life in human form on Earth impact His teachings while here?

Jesus lived on Earth as unto the Law. In all aspects, He lived under the Law perfectly. That included tithing and His pronouncements while here.

Following all the requirements of the Law, His perfect life fulfilled the Law perfectly, making Him the only true, worthy sacrifice for the benefit of all.

As to Jesus and tithing, there are several examples that show Jesus tithed while on Earth:

- He ate with Pharisees who would never have eaten with Him had he not tithed (Luke 7).

- He commended the woman who tithed her two mites (Mark 12:41–44).

- He also criticized Pharisees' focus on tithing to the exclusion of everything else.

While these verses would tend to suggest Jesus was carrying tithing into the New Testament, He wasn't doing that at all. Jesus lived His whole life on Earth under the Old Testament to fulfill the Old Testament to be a sacrifice for all.

His success in fulfilling the Law made Him a worthy sacrifice for all, satisfying God the Father's perfect justice and opening the path for a right relationship between God and man.

For Jesus, whether to tithe or not was settled. He was a Jew under the Law, and such people tithed. Here, He put it in context: yes, tithe, but don't get legalistic about it. Especially don't focus on it and neglect the more important things: justice, mercy, and faith. These words still apply today.

That is not to make tithing an insignificant thing. Read Malachi 3:10 again, and realize tithing is important to God too.

Finally, Pentecost signified the beginning of that marvelous relationship, allowing God the Holy Spirit to come and live inside of man, to guide, prompt, convict, and comfort us in our everyday lives, all to the glory of God.

God counseled and fellowshipped with Adam and Eve in the garden. The Fall changed that. God and man were separated thereafter up until the cross and resurrection. With the issue of sin being wiped away, we now have an opportunity through God's grace and our faith in His Son, to live a complete, wonderful life.

The Law and the requirement for tithing are not legally required anymore, but they remain a better way to live in principle. Again, the 10 Commandments have not lost their righteous guidance. Neither has tithing been repealed as a method for God blessing us.

Points To Consider:

God has always wanted to love us, even in the times of our most despicable thoughts and acts. Jesus was the bridge, the link to provide us a way to a vibrant, ongoing relationship.

Even when we mess up, He has provided confession to the believer and a cleansing of our unrighteousness. He doesn't want punishment; He wants the downtime in our relationship to be as short as possible. Hurry and get back on track.

Who else can love you like that? Glory to God! Thank you, Jesus, for making this possible!

How Was Tithing Impacted by the Crucifixion and Resurrection?

"For my yoke is easy and my burden is light."
—Matthew 11:30

The above verse is talking about our relationship with Jesus while He was on Earth but also, more importantly, our relationship with Him after His death on the cross and His resurrection.

For the Godhead (Father, Son, and Holy Spirit), as well as for all mankind, the completion of that fateful weekend was massive, spectacular, long-awaited—I could go on with more superlative adjectives, but you get the picture—seismic shift in relationship between God and man.

For an unknown time period, God had been limited in His ability to interact with mankind. He didn't create Adam and Eve so they could be ostracized or avoided. God the Father wanted a loving, enjoyable relationship with His greatest creation.

And that weekend, it became possible! The sin barrier was overcome and the chasm between God and man was bridged through the saving grace of our Savior, Jesus Christ.

In the morning, Jesus met with Mary Magdalene in the garden. He told her He could not be touched because He hadn't gone to the Father. That night, He ate dinner with people who must have at some point touched Him.

What happened during that day? The answer is found in Daniel 7:13–14:

> In my vision at night I looked, and there before me was one like a son of man [referring to Jesus], coming with the clouds of heaven. He approached the Ancient of Days [God the Father] and was led into his presence. He was given authority, glory and sovereign power; all nations and peoples of every language worshiped him. His dominion is an everlasting dominion that will not pass away, and his kingdom is one that will never be destroyed.

He started out the day in a tomb, had a triumphal return in Heaven, and then met two disciples on the way to Emmaus, had dinner on Earth, and then disappeared.

I would call that a big day.

So, how did Jesus' relationship to man change? More importantly for this book, how was tithing changed for the New Testament believer?

No more was the Law the focus of God's interaction with man. Jesus had paid the price for all mankind. And what was the price for man in this arrangement? Believing everything Jesus said about who He was and why He was here. That is amazing grace!

The currency for activating grace? Faith. Faith in Jesus is what grace makes available.

So, what about tithing? Tithing is no longer required by law because the Law has been replaced. You are no longer required to keep strict accounts and give a set percentage of your income.

Unless you want to.

I want to. As I've said, Carol and I have tithed since 1996. In doing so, our finances have flourished, our marriage has strengthened, our kids and their spouses love the Lord, and our grandkids are healthy and thriving. God has blessed us in innumerable ways. Relying on His promise in Malachi 3:10 has been the basis of all these blessings, I have no doubt.

Again, the promise He makes in the verse has never been repealed. It is another way to take His word in faith in Him and His love, the currency that activates God's grace: "What is important is faith expressing itself in love" (Galatians 5:6 NLT).

It is available to you too, believer in Christ.

Points To Consider:

Today, we don't tithe under compulsion, we tithe because we know it pleases God, and we know it still is rewarded.

The reward does not come from the amount; it comes from the faith and obedience we show in Him and His word. His word is a promise that extends into the church age.

The difference between Old Testament tithing and New Testament tithing is that in the Old Testament, tithing was compulsory. Now, as noted in Galatians 5:6, tithing is a way to express our love and faith in Him.

Is it the only way? The best way? Certainly not, but it is a really good way because God has made promises to bless tithing, and those promises still hold true.

What is The Right Relationship with God?

In the church age, our sins no longer separate us from God the Father. Jesus Christ's sacrifice on the cross broke the barrier between God and man caused by sin. No longer are Christians (people who have accepted Christ's gift to us on the cross) separated from God by our sins.

Believers have Jesus' sacrifice credited to them, so when God sees us, He doesn't see our falling but our identification with Christ and His perfection. This allows God, the God of love and so much more, to deal with us in love with His perfect justice satisfied.

Now, as part of our right relationship with God, let's figure out how to comply.

Christians believe that Jesus Christ is the promise fulfilled that was prophesied throughout the Old Testament. Still, there are aspects of the Old Testament that remain very vital in our lives. None of the 10 Commandments were repealed. You should honor your parents and not commit murder or covet or steal, even another's wife. All the Commandments provide the most excellent ways to live our lives. Proverbs and Psalms have not been repealed but amplify a right way to go through life. The Old Testament provides an excellent background to the Gospels and the New Covenant we now live under.

So too does Malachi 3, which provides a proper understanding of Old Testament giving. The passage culminates in what God means when He says, "you rob me."

So, what about now, in the church age?

With sin no longer separating us from the Trinity, we can lose ourselves in God's love. What do I mean by that? God wants to bless us more than we can ask or think (Ephesians 3:20–21). The key is giving Him room in our daily lives so we can experience, enjoy, and be edified by all the wonderful blessings He wants to share.

Will there be difficulties? Most definitely, but with difficulties, there is growth for the believer who leans on the Lord during hard times. Difficulties mature us, and you grow while under pressure. I want to know Him amid my sufferings, which will surely come (Philippians 3:10).

My job is to maintain what our Lord has already obtained. I want to submit to God, stand in His word, and cause the Devil to flee from me, my family, my community, and my nation. The shield of my faith is the word of God.

And where is tithing in all this? From His words, I know He blesses faith. From faith, I can confidently tithe to my local church, knowing the outreach to those in need will be extensive and effective. I know that tithing is the vehicle to leverage my outreach and in doing so, I will receive blessings from Him.

I have practiced tithing long enough to know it works. I have the promise of God that He will bless me for tithing. I have seen it too many times in my life to doubt. He loves my faith in giving, and He loves that I have joined in the effort to edify the church and to help others.

Tithing has enriched my family, my marriage, and my life because I have undertaken this in faith in His word.

His word is true.

Points To Consider:

Okay, we have gotten to the grabber: I have laid out my understanding of tithing, applied it to my life despite any potential objections, and it has been incredible in every aspect of my existence.

I am asking you to jump off that diving board with the faith of a four-year-old. Try it. You'll like it.

Grace and Faith

What do Shadrach, Meshach, and Abednego in the fiery furnace, Daniel in the lion's den, Saul's thorn in his side, and Danny and Carol Crain in their times of financial difficulties have in common?

God was with them during all their trials.

Being a child of God does not eliminate trials and desperate times. What it does is remind you who is in charge, who loves you, and who promises to be with you constantly in times of trouble.

Discomfort, even terror, is used to mature us in our reliance on Him. You must grow and you grow during times of pressure. You are not promised that you won't experience stress or discomfort or worse. You are promised He will be with you always, even in the darkest hour.

When you face discomfort or uncertain times and pressure, He promises to be there with you. When you first start tithing, having not seen God's faithfulness in your life, it can be kind of scary. I remember those days were a little tentative and uncertain but exciting at the same time, knowing from His word that He promised certain things, and I could count on Him. He always performed beyond expectations. He still does, and it is much easier for me to believe now.

Financial stress is uncomfortable. It is a constant pain. But when you rely on God, that discomfort matures you and allows you to grow in your reliance on the Lord, while being blessed in your obedience. I'm telling you it has been a blessing to increase my leaning into God. I start every day with a prayer of "Lord, I am depending on you today." I can say that prayer in faith today because of the nearly 30 years of tithing, in faith, I have experienced.

I want to know Christ—yes, to know the power of his resurrection
and participation in his sufferings, becoming like him in his death,
and so, somehow, attaining to the resurrection from the dead.

—Philippians 3:10–11

These verses require faith in Him and faith in His gift on the cross. That faith translates into every aspect of our lives to enrich us here, and then, we're off to Heaven. Faith, like muscle building, grows the most through stress and adversity. Muscle building is not pleasant during the act, but the reward follows. Build your faith up in the process of relying on Him more and more through all times, good and bad. No longer be the one double minded about Jesus and His intent for you. Grow in your faith. Access His grace. Grab every aspect of the gifts attained in His resurrection.

> All praise to God, the Father of our Lord Jesus Christ. God is our merciful Father and the source of all comfort. He comforts us in all our troubles so that we can comfort others. When they are troubled, we will be able to give them the same comfort God has given us. For the more we suffer for Christ, the more God will shower us with his comfort through Christ. Even when we are weighed down with troubles, it is for your comfort and salvation! For when we ourselves are comforted, we will certainly comfort you. Then you can patiently endure the same things we suffer. We are confident that as you share in our sufferings, you will also share in the comfort God gives us (2 Corinthians 1:3–7 NLT).

When you lean into God during times of trouble, He gives you His presence, comfort, and patience. This is a time of growth. Growing muscles are painful but powerful. Spiritual muscles are the same. Bulk up in the Lord so that you can help others while you are edified. God is using this time for your good and you will be blessed as you come through it. "Let all that I am wait quietly before God, for my hope is in Him" (Psalm 62:5 NLT).

Four Examples of God's Grace in People's Lives During Discomfort

All the people described above faced serious trouble and dramatic potential consequences, including loss of life—being thrown into a fiery furnace, facing the prospect of being eaten by lions, living with a continuous pain in his side, and facing financial hardship like the people above were facing. God intervened in all these troubles but did not immediately resolve them. He used each of these situations to strengthen the people in their trauma and caused them to rely on Him.

He was with each of these people through grace during their time of terror and/or pain. Each came out more spiritually mature, relying on the Father more often and more deeply.

Here's what Paul said in 2 Corinthians 12:5–10:

> I will boast about a man like that, but I will not boast about myself, except about my weaknesses. Even if I should choose to boast, I would not be a fool, because I would be speaking the truth. But I refrain, so no one will think more of me than is warranted by what I do or say, or because of these surpassingly great revelations. Therefore, in order to keep me from becoming conceited, I was given a thorn in my flesh, a messenger of Satan, to torment me. Three times I pleaded with the Lord to take it away from me. But he said to me, "My grace is sufficient for you, for my power is made perfect in weakness." Therefore I will boast all the more gladly about my weaknesses, so that Christ's power may rest on me. That is why, for Christ's sake, I delight in weaknesses, in insults, in hardships, in persecutions, in difficulties. For when I am weak, then I am strong.

Wow! This is strong! The man who wrote more than half of the New Testament faced a thorn in the flesh, a constant pain that he lifted up to God at least three times. God showed that an ever-present pain can improve our reliance on God, so we become ever more reliant on Him, making us closer to the Deity who loves us.

To obtain this closeness and maintain a relationship tied into Christ's power, Paul gladly traded the pain for a right relationship with our Lord.

124

I don't know about you but there have been times of absolute confusion and pain and despair that can only be comforted by the close presence of God in my thoughts, prayers, and His word. During those times, even if seemingly helpless, I know the Lord will fix the instant trial and calamity, that He will protect me, and that if I can remain strong in Him, my relationship with Him will grow, be stronger, and prepare me for a more blessed future.

I have had a lot of impossible, dire, or scary situations in my life, but none has ever sunk me, not because of my talents but because I have learned to lean into the Lord.

As to how this interacts with tithing, I believe that I cannot outgive God. If that is the case, and it is, I never have to worry that He will leave me stranded. He loves me, and He loves when I turn to Him, even in abject depressing situations.

As Paul said in 2 Corinthians 12:9: "But he said to me, 'My grace is sufficient for you, for my power is made perfect in weakness.' Therefore I will boast all the more gladly about my weaknesses, so that Christ's power may rest on me."

I am quite happy about "the thorn," and about insults and hardships, persecutions and difficulties, for when I am weak, then I am strong. Believe me, as I have gotten older, the faith to rest in His protection has gotten easier. He has never let me down. Has He resolved things differently than I have requested? Almost always. Has His ways proved better? Every time.

Why am I telling these incidents? Because God was with each one of us during our trials. He didn't take them away, but He was with us as things worked out, helping us become more spiritually mature as we relied more on Him. When the discomfort and terror were over, and the constant pain Paul felt either subsided or was tolerated, do you think any of us came out the same?

Carol and I being stretched financially numerous times or facing other serious difficulties is small potatoes compared to the historic calamities of these heroes of the faith; nevertheless, the principles are the same. He won't necessarily rid you of the trial and discomfort, but He will provide you with grace and strength while you are in it.

Indeed, don't you know seeing the Lord walking around with them in the fiery furnace was an overwhelming experience? How about being surrounded by hungry lions and having the peace to fall asleep? Think of Paul's exhilaration to suffer if it meant relying more on God's grace?

I hope I have communicated the wonder we have felt from the personal touch of God on our finances through tithing that has spread into our whole lives and is now growing in our children and grandchildren. God's grace continues to bless us supernaturally daily. Discomfort will come, but it allows us to grow in faith and see His grace. Grow like Paul and learn how to embrace it.

Points To Consider:

Psalm 23:3–4: "He refreshes my soul. He guides me along the right paths for his name's sake. Even though I walk through the darkest valley, I will fear no evil, for you are with me; your rod and your staff, they comfort me."

Think of the Biblical heroes described above. God didn't always remove the challenge they faced, but He was right there with them, to strengthen, console, and advise them as they walked through their challenges. Overcoming a challenge in fellowship with God is one of the great feelings one can experience.

Think of times in your life where you overcame a challenge by the strength of God.

Life in the Old Testament Versus New Testament Living

A few points to know:

The Law points the way to the fact that there is no hope in ourselves for salvation. No one was worthy as the sacrifice for all have sinned. As such, we needed and need now a Savior.

That Savior is Jesus Christ. He came for salvation. He came to show us the way to live an outstanding, blessed life by following the promptings and guidance of the Holy Spirit (be sensitive to the Holy Spirit in your life, for you should depend on God always, every day).

That is what faith at its best is and what offers your best life by staying in right relationship with God, which is why He ultimately sent Jesus to die for us because He wanted a love-filled relationship with the likes of you and me. Again, praise God!

How does this work? The Holy Spirit teaches us how to live, prompts us to do right in our daily life, warns us about the course we are taking, puts us back on the right path when we sin, and strengthens us to learn the better way as we get on the right path in our daily lives. The Holy Spirit shows us the better way, making sin so much less attractive than it was before the indwelling of the Holy Spirit. The Holy Spirit gives us life and gives it to us more abundantly (John 10:10).

The Law was never meant to do that. Jesus was always the source of creation and life. Jesus provides life to us through our faith in Him and empowers us through the Holy Spirit to align our lives towards God's plan for our lives and please Him more each day, as we grow in our relationship with Him.

In the Old Testament, compliance with the Jewish Law stemmed from fear, not only of punishment but of lost blessings. God blessed those who followed the Law and did not bless those who did not follow the Law. In essence, the Law limited God's ability to show His love to the Jews because of their actions.

The Law was given by Moses, a sinful man, to a sinful race. Jesus, the Son of God, became the Son of Man so that the sons of man could become the sons of God.

In the New Testament, the whole weight of sin and its destructiveness was put on Jesus. Now, because Jesus has paid the price, God is no longer limited by our imperfections in blessing us. When God sees the New Testament believer, He sees Christ in us. Sin is no longer the issue because it has been paid for.

Our relationship with God can flourish because we are no longer separated by the barrier of sin. You still sin occasionally, but you have the blessing from Jesus' work on the cross and the avenue to get right with God quickly: "If we confess our sins, He is faithful and just to forgive us our sins and to cleanse us from all unrighteousness" (1 John 1:9 NKJV).

Confess and keep moving. The dad doesn't hold the stumbles against the child or spank him for falling. Sure, there might be some consequences from the fall, like a skinned knee, but the Father doesn't punish. Rather, the dad works to correct the child's walk and helps to get the child down the road.

Stay on the path and out of love for God, try to cut down on the stumbles and improve your walk in righteousness.

Points To Consider:

Hebrews 10:16–17: "This is the covenant I will make with them after that time, says the Lord. I will put my laws in their hearts, and I will write them on their minds… Their sins and lawless acts I will remember no more."

How does God no longer choose to remember the lawless acts of the believer?

How does God put His laws on the heart of a New Testament believer?

What role in the above verses is performed by the Holy Spirit, God in us?

So, consider this:

After thousands of years of people wandering around aimlessly and out of fellowship, God chose a people to show the world who He was and what He could do for them.

Ultimately, this was put into the Law that (1) showed everyone, including His chosen people, that no one could follow all the laws and (2) that they needed a Savior to put them fully right with God for all time.

The perfect lamb, Jesus, completed His sacrifice, which freed people to accept salvation found in Him.

After His death and resurrection, on Pentecost, the Holy Spirit came to indwell in those who believed in Christ and accepted His wonderful gift.

With the indwelling of the Holy Spirit, God is permanently in us. He is a prompter, a guide, a warning, a comforter, a celebrator when we honor Christ, and a griever when we deny or violate the desires of the Godhead with our acts and intents that dishonor Him. Yet, He is always ready to accept our confession and contrition and to move on in our relationship.

> He is the one who has helped us tell others about his new agreement to save them. We do not tell them that they must obey every law of God or die; but we tell them there is life for them from the Holy Spirit. The old way, trying to be saved by keeping the Ten Commandments, ends in death; in the new way, the Holy Spirit gives them life (2 Corinthians 3:6 TLB).

Does the Bible Say Christians Must Tithe?

In a word: No.

Tithing was required in the Old Testament for the support of the church leaders and the poor. New Testament Christians are called to give according to 2 Corinthians 9:6–7 (MSG): "Remember: A stingy planter gets a stingy crop; a lavish planter gets a lavish crop. I want each of you to take plenty of time to think it over, and make up your own mind what you will give. That will protect you against sob stories and arm-twisting. God loves it when the giver delights in the giving." This is the joy of living in the New Testament age.

If this is the standard for what to give, then give from the heart what delights you. Make up your own mind. While I certainly do not advocate that believers are required to tithe to please God, I certainly know that you are missing out if you don't. God's word in Malachi 3:10 has not been revised or overturned. Test Him in this, He says, and see if blessings do not overflow to you. That is not me talking. It's God—the One who never changes (Malachi 3:6)—saying it and it still applies today.

Take another look at verses 6–7 above: "A stingy planter gets a stingy crop; a lavish planter gets a lavish crop."

The New Testament age is so awesome. We have the blessings of God in human form dying on the cross so that we can live a great life and then go to Heaven. That beats anything in the Old Testament. He wants you to live in the lavish category. How do you get there? By faith in the One who died on the cross to make all this possible. Don't limit Him and His blessings to your demonstrated faith; be lavish in your faith (including daily faith in the Holy Spirit's guidance)! Give lavishly, even more than 10%! It's not the money He seeks. He wants faith demonstrated. That is how you please God and that is how He rewards you the most and the best!

If you get nothing else out of this book, buy into this last paragraph.

What Happened With the Arrival of the New Testament Age?

Jesus' gift on the cross and His resurrection made the following possible for all.

> For if, by the trespass of the one man, death reigned through that one man, how much more will those who receive God's abundant provision of grace and of the gift of righteousness reign in life through the one man, Jesus Christ!
>
> Consequently, just as one trespass resulted in condemnation for all people, so also one righteous act resulted in justification and life for all people. For just as through the disobedience of the one man the many were made sinners, so also through the obedience of the one man the many will be made righteous.
>
> The law was brought in so that the trespass might increase. But where sin increased, grace increased all the more, so that, just as sin reigned in death, so also grace might reign through righteousness to bring eternal life through Jesus Christ our Lord (Romans 5:17–21).

Jesus' death and resurrection eliminated the sin barrier that kept God and man apart, opening the way for grace to be the operating system in the New Testament for how God deals with man. Glory to God!

Look, God knows even the most beautiful, smartest, strongest, or compassionate person is nothing more than dust… and He loves all of us anyway. Jesus' saving grace allows God to bless us any way He wants and as often as He wants. Our merit isn't an issue; our works are filthy rags and still He wants to love on us every day!

To access His grace is to increase, verbalize, and stand on our faith in Him. His word is alive and powerful and available for you to grow in and stand on as it contains His promises.

Even the best Old Testament believers were servants. Abraham, Isaac, and Jacob are referred to as servants (Exodus 32:13). Even Moses was a faithful servant to God (Hebrews 3:5), yet you, New Testament believer, are His son (John 1:11–12).

In the Old Testament, God was referred to as the "judge." This is said in part because man related to God through the Law because compliance with the Law's requirements was the way to interacting with God. When you sin, you make the appropriate sacrifice for the sin you committed, then when you were atoned for, you approached God.

The New Testament changed that in two ways.

First, Jesus atoned once and for all for all sins (including those committed in the 20th, 21st, and 22nd centuries and so on) for all people who accepted His glorious gift to them, even if He never met them face to face. Now, there are no more lambs being sacrificed at the church.

Second, He brought into the God-man relationship the Holy Spirit as the administrator of our interaction with the Godhead (Father-Son-Holy Spirit). The Holy Spirit operates under what He has heard from the Father and reflects the glory and power of the Son. He is the third person of the Trinity—our comforter, helper, advisor, advocate, umpire, empowerer, teacher, and guide.

Ask God in prayer early in the morning what needs to be done and how should it be done, and then ask for His guidance to accomplish all things in your day. That's about the best way to start your day.

This is the administration of our lives the way God intended in the garden—a vibrant interaction with us always leaning into Him. He makes everything available to us and by faith, we grab it and stay in His will and power until the task or achievement is completed. We are blessed by activating the grace He makes available by our faith in Him. He gets the glory!

We stumble; we confess and get back on track. Together with God in faith, we conquer and succeed.

Have I given you any indication that any of the marvelous, outrageous, wonderful things that have happened in my life have come through self-effort? I am not that smart, and I don't have that kind of foresight.

What I have done is take God at His word as it relates to my finances, giving a tenth at a minimum of my income and increase. God has graced me with the rest of the incredible blessings He has bestowed.

We are blessed to be living now in the New Testament age with a loving God who deals with us through grace, not the Law. Grow in His grace and live your best life now.

Tithing is a great way to please God, not by compliance to an old law but by demonstrating tangibly your faith in His promise in Malachi 3:10! He said it. I do it. Things work out great in all aspects of my life because I take Him at His word. He does not disappoint. My life is not perfect, and I have my challenges like everybody does, but I have a lot more peace, a lot more blessings, and a lot better sense of how much He loves me. Tithing is the source of nearly everything claimed in that last paragraph.

I recommend it highly.

However you proceed, give from the heart. In the New Testament Age, He wants you to give from the heart, from the effect your redemption has had on you, your love for him.

Your giving communicates your love and thanks and honors the totality of His awesomeness in your life. Abraham gave before the Law was implemented. His giving of 10% was from his heart, not the Law, and God honored it. Whatever you give and whatever much you give, do it in a manner that communicates your love and honors Him.

SCAN HERE to learn more about
Invite Ministries—created to invite people to a deeper
faith and living relationship with Jesus Christ